Volume II

READINGS IN
RUSSIAN HISTORY

Alexander V. Riasanovsky
University of Pennsylvania

William E. Watson
Temple University

KENDALL/HUNT PUBLISHING COMPANY
2460 Kerper Boulevard P.O. Box 539 Dubuque, Iowa 52004-0539

Excerpts from *Imperial Russia: A Source Book 1700–1917,* Second Edition by Basil Dmystryshyn, Copyright © 1974 by Holt, Rinehart and Winston, Inc., reprinted by permission of the publisher.

Acknowledgement is due to Martin Gilbert and George Weidenfeld & Nicolson Ltd. for permission to reproduce the maps on pages 171–175 taken from the Russian History Atlas.

Library of Congress Catalog Card Number: 91–62648

ISBN 0–8403–7160–8

Printed in the United States of America
10 9 8 7 6 5 4 3 2

Contents

preface **vii**

PART ONE ❖ RUSSIAN HISTORY IN
THE EIGHTEENTH CENTURY

Chapter One: The Age of Peter the Great

Introduction **5**
The Table of Ranks **11**
Peter's Decrees on the Duties of the Senate **12**
Letter from Peter to the Holy Synod **13**
Peter's Instruction to Russian Students Abroad Studying Navigation **14**
The Story of the Ship's-Boat **15**
Baptism **20**
Voltaire's View of Peter's Russia **25**
The Funeral Oration of Archbishop Theophanes for Peter the Great **32**

Chapter Two: Anna and Elizabeth

Introduction **37**
Anna's Accession **41**
The Empress Elizabeth **44**

Chapter Three: Catherine the Great and the Enlightenment

Introduction   47
Catherine's Official Title   51
Catherine on Her Wedding Day   51
Catherine and the Gubernias   53
Catherine's Epitaph, Composed by Herself   53
The Manifesto on the Freedom of the Nobility   54
The Charter of the Rights, Freedoms, and Privileges of the Noble Russian
   Dvorianstvo   54
S. E. Desnitskii's Proposal on the Division of Powers   55
Edicts of Pugachev   56
Testimony from Pugachev's Interrogation at Iaik Town   58
The Institution of the Administration of the Provinces of the Empire   61
The Nakaz   63
Suvorov's Art of Victory   65
Radishchev on the Peasants   66

Chapter Four: Paul

Introduction   67
Paul's Coronation   69
Formalities at Paul's Court   70
The Assassination of Paul   71

PART TWO ✧ RUSSIAN HISTORY IN THE NINETEENTH AND EARLY TWENTIETH CENTURIES

Chapter Five: Alexander I: Reform and the Napoleonic Invasion

Introduction   77
Alexander's Education   81
Alexander's Plans of Reform and the Ministries   81
The Ministry of Public Instruction   84
The Unofficial Committee   85
Alexander's Disillusionment with Napoleon   87
The Suffering of the People Wrought by Napoleon's Invasion   87
Alexander's Address to His Troops on the Rhine   88
Alexander's Address to the Aldermen of the City of Paris   89
Alexander's Proclamation Upon Entering Paris   89
Kutuzov, According to the French   90
"Alas, Poor Buonaparte"   91

The Earl of Liverpool's Address   92
Karamzin's Conservative Vision   93

Chapter Six: Nicholas I: Reactionary Rule and the Crimean War

Introduction   95
The Grand Duke Constantine   99
A Letter from Nicholas to Constantine   100
The Decembrists and Their Appeal   100
A Decembrist Manifesto Written by "Dictator" Trubetskoi   103
*The Proclamation of the Southern Society, Written by Serge Ivanovich
   Murav'ev-Apostol*   104
The Habits of Nicholas I   105
Russian Wildlife   106
Golovine on the Nobility   108
Background to the Crimean War: the Conflict over the Shrines   110
Queen Victoria's Declaration of War   113
The Horrors of the Front Line   114
The Allies and the Treaty of Paris   116

Chapter Seven: Alexander II and Emancipation

Introduction   117
A Description of Alexander II   121
Von Haxthausen on the Mir   122
*The Necessity of Emancipation: Alexander's Address to the Nobles
   in Moscow*   123
The Emancipation Manifesto   123
*Russian Emancipation Viewed from the Confederate States of
   America*   124
Russian Emancipation, According to Northern U.S. Newspapers   125
*Alexander on the Need for Further Reform: His Address to
   the Nobles*   126
The Sale of Russian America   127
The Future of Russia, from Herzen's Memoirs   129
Ivan Aksakov on the Assassination of Alexander II   130
A French Diplomat's Remarks at the Funeral of Alexander II   131

Chapter Eight: Alexander III and the Rise of Russian Radicalism

Introduction   133

The Character and Habits of Alexander III, According to
   Serge Witte **137**
The Construction of the Trans-Siberian Railroad **138**
Looking for Work in Russian Industry **139**
Marx: Russia and Revolution **140**
Lenin on the Need for Activism **140**
The Death of Alexander III **141**

Chapter Nine: Nicholas II and the Twilight of Imperial Russia

Introduction **143**
The Coronation of Nicholas II **149**
Pobedonostsev on the Press **150**
Nicholas II and Japan **151**
The Russo-Japanese War **152**
The Vodka Monopoly During the Russo-Japanese War **153**
Bloody Sunday **154**
The 1905 Revolution **157**
Witte's "Loan That Saved Russia" **161**
Stolypin's Land Reform **164**
Stolypin on Population Growth **166**
Rasputin in St. Petersburg **166**
The Secret Telegram Sent by the Russian Ambassador in France, Izvolsky,
   to the Russian Foreign Secretary, Sazonov **167**
Nicholas II on the Outbreak of the First World War: His Remarks to the
   Duma Members and the State Council in the Winter Palace **168**
Domestic Difficulties in War Time: A Police Report **169**
An Eye-Witness to Anti-Tsarist Soldiers Marching in Petrograd **170**

Appendix: Maps **171**
Questions to Consider **176**
Glossary **179**
Bibliography **180**

Preface

We have endeavored in Volume Two of *Readings in Russian History* to achieve the same goal we set forth in Volume One, namely, to provide students of Russian history with sources in translation which discuss both the great events of "macrohistory" and the details of "microhistory." While textbooks provide students of history with an analysis of broad historical processes, this anthology makes accessible to instructors and students the kind of texts which reveal the "human element." We believe that many of the texts which we have chosen illuminate individual human existence more clearly than texts used in other anthologies of its type. The selections written by Johann-Georg Korb and Ivan Golovine concerning religious, cultural, and social customs of eighteenth and nineteenth-century Russia, for example, are unique "time capsules" to aid the instructor and student in recreating this historical landscape of Russia more accurately than many of the texts containing "macrohistorical" facts.

Volume One of *Readings in Russian History* contained a chapter devoted to early foreign observations of Russia, and included material of a cross-cultural interest in several other chapters. We have endeavored in Volume Two to produce the same results by including Western observations about Russia in the reign of Peter the Great, when a host of Western influences took hold in certain segments of Russian society, to reveal the true parameters of that influence. Similarly, we have provided the reader with texts on the impact of the Napoleonic invasion under Alexander I from the perspectives of the Russians, the French, and Russia's Western allies, the British (from contemporary editions of the London Times).

Chronologically, Volume Two begins with the reign of Peter the Great (1689–1725), and concludes with the stirrings of discontent in the reign of Nicholas II. Volume Three will begin with Russian involvement in the First World War and the Revolution(s) of 1917 and conclude with the dramatic events of December 1989 and August 1991. Very important symbols of the imperial Russian world, as presented in this volume, have reemerged as this book goes to press. Above all, it appears to be the symbols which were created by Peter the Great which have caught the imagination of the recent Russian revolutionaries: the tsarist tri-color flag flown by those backing Boris Yeltsin was designed by Peter, and the old imperial capital of St. Petersburg, renamed Leningrad after the charismatic Bolshevik leader Vladimir I. Lenin, has had its name restored recently by its citizens in a referendum approved by the Russian Parliament.

The editors assume full responsibility for any errors (or virtues) inherent to the volumes. As in any collaboration, there was a division of labor in this project. Dr. Alexander V. Riasanovsky has lectured in Russian history for over thirty years at the University of Pennsylvania, and as guest lecturer at Stanford, Harvard, Princeton, Swarthmore, Bryn Mawr and other institutions. On the basis of that experience, he chose the documents included in the volumes. Dr. William E. Watson served as Dr. Riasanovsky's teaching assistant at the University of Pennsylvania and as his preceptor at Princeton University, and wrote the introductions to the texts in the volumes. The introductions are not intended in any way to replace a textbook. Rather, they are explanations for students of the individual passages in each section. As a result of our experience in lecturing and leading discussion sections, we believe that we have indeed found those texts which have been most effective in communicating the experience of Russia to students. The variations in spelling, transliteration, and capitalization which are found in the texts used in this volume result from the differences in style utilized by the various translators whose works we have selected.

x

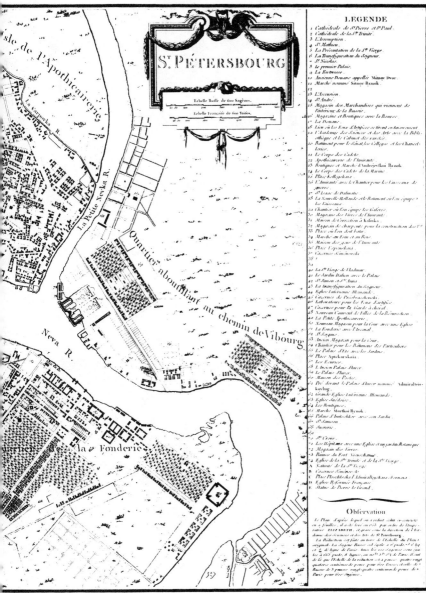

Reproduced in 1965 by *HISTORIC URBAN PLANS*, Ithaca, New York

This is number   of an edition limited to 500 copies

Volume II

READINGS IN
RUSSIAN
HISTORY

PART ONE

✤

Russian History in the Eighteenth Century

Photo: The Kremlin Walls and St. Basil's Cathedral in Moscow.

Photo: The Winter Palace and the Alexander Column in St. Petersburg.

CHAPTER ONE
The Age of Peter the Great

CHAPTER TWO
Anna and Elizabeth

CHAPTER THREE
*Catherine the Great
and the Enlightenment*

CHAPTER FOUR
Paul

Chapter One

THE AGE OF
PETER THE GREAT

*The significance of the reforms initiated by
Peter I Romanov (1689–1725) have constituted
one of the greatest problems in Russian histo-
riography for over two centuries. Considering
his reign to be the pivotal point in Russian history, many scholars have traditionally divided Russian history into distinct pre- and post-Petrine periods.
The Senate which Peter created in 1711 to assume administrative duties in
his absence bestowed the lasting epithet of "the Great" upon him in 1721,
following the signing of the Treaty of Nystadt (concluding Russia's victory
over Sweden in the Great Northern War). Various assessments of his career,
however, have been given by some of the principal figures in Russian political and cultural history, and reflect the ambivalence felt by Russians since
his reign: Lomonosov called Peter a "god-like man;" Miliukov called Peter's reforms the "necessary outcome of a logical development;" Karamzin
wrote that, because of Peter's reforms, Russians "began to be citizens of the
world; but we ceased in some measure to be citizens of Russia;" Stalin said
that Peter "accomplished a great deal toward the creation and strengthen-
ing of the national state of the landowners and merchants . . . at the expense
of the serf peasantry."*

*Peter journeyed to Western Europe in 1697–98 in order to forge political
alliances and to acquire much-needed maritime and military technology. The
subsequent revamping of the Russian army in 1705 was inevitably patterned
on Western models, and some historians have argued that many of his other
reforms resulted from a desire to Westernize: the creation of administrative
departments called colleges within the government; the creation of the Holy
Synod to direct the Russian Orthodox Church; the legislation enacted to tax
traditional aspects of Russian attire (long beards, hats, robes); the adoption
of the Gregorian calendar; and the construction of Peter's "Window on the
West," the new European-style capital of the empire on the Neva River, St.
Petersburg. Peter, however, did not set out simply to emulate the West.
Rather, he took from the West what he felt was necessary to modernize Russia in order to transform the nation into a great power. Some historians,
such as Kliuchevsky, have argued that Russian culture changed little as a
result of Peter's reforms. While the nobility increasingly came to adopt
Western customs, language (German and French in particular), and styles of
dress, especially in St. Petersburg and Moscow, the overwhelming majority*

of Peter's subjects, the peasantry, remained virtually unchanged (according to the first census in Russian history, taken by Peter in 1710, the population of the empire at this time was thirteen million, and the peasants comprised perhaps eighty-five percent of the total). It must also be noted when assessing his reforms that Peter brought crushing burdens on the peasants in new requirements for military service and in his various construction projects (over one hundred thousand laborers, for example, perished in the construction of St. Petersburg).

A continuing topic of debate is whether Peter should more correctly be referred to as a "modernizer" rather than as a "Westernizer." For instance, some scholars have argued that certain reforms traditionally considered to be Western in origin actually have non-Western sources. An example of the latter is the suggestion that the Turkish divan is the ultimate source of the college system initiated by Peter, rather than a Western model such as the Swedish Lutheran synodal apparatus of ecclesiastical organization. In addition, Peter set a number of Russian boys to learning Japanese, and may have (perhaps prematurely) "hedged his bets."

Peter introduced the Table of Ranks in 1722 to create a loyal service nobility supportive of his reforms. The Table of Ranks was the means by which non-noble landowners could attain a title of nobility through service in the imperial civil service or army. The first passage in this section is the Table of Ranks, translated by Basil Dmytryshyn. Many of the titles held by the nobility at this time were Western in origin in imitation of the title of emperor (Latin imperator) bestowed on Peter by the Senate, which he preferred to that of tsar'.

Peter created the Senate to assume the administrative duties of the imperial government while he was away from the capital, especially when he was on one of his many military campaigns. Our second selection consists of Peter's decrees on the duties of the Senate (translated by Dmytryshyn). His interest in military affairs went beyond the restructuring of the army, and Peter was interested in personally commanding Russian forces on campaigns. Our third passage is a letter written by Peter while on campaign to the Caspian city of Darband, addressed to the Holy Synod (taken from an early English translation made in 1729 by Thomas Consett, the Anglican chaplin to resident English merchants in Moscow).

For economic and military purposes, Peter was interested in improving the maritime capabilities of Russia. Early in his reign Peter introduced the first imperial Russian navy (1695), and one of the priorities of his journey to the West was the acquisition of maritime technology (with some of which he personally acquainted himself). Peter sent a number of Russian students abroad to acquire modern technical skills, in order to create modern weapons and munitions factories. Our fourth passage is Peter's "Instruction to Russian Students Abroad Studying Navigation" (translated by Dmytryshyn). The fifth passage is Consett's translation of "The Story of the Ship's-Boat," which is said by the translator to have given Peter "the thought of building ships of war."

A number of Western historians, especially of the Soviet period, have underemphasized the role played by religion in the shaping of what may be termed "Russia's national character." Towards the end of the twentieth century, however, there has been a large-scale religious revival within the Soviet Union. The most notable aspects of this revival have been the tremendous increase in Russian Orthodox congregations, the reopening of churches once closed by the Soviet government, the construction of new churches, and most recently, the celebration of the Orthodox Liturgy within the Kremlin itself. Other faiths have likewise shown remarkable growth and resiliance. Consequently, it seems appropriate, even vital to offer an eyewitness account of Russian religious practices during the reign of Peter the Great (who was not noted as a close friend of established religion). Our sixth passage is taken from the diary of Johann-Georg Korb, who was an Austrian Secretary of Legation at Peter's court. The excerpts which we have selected from Korb's diary contain revealing information concerning Russian religious practices in the age of Peter the Great. The diary was translated into English by the Count MacDonnell, and it suggests that the changes which did occur in Russia as a result of Peter's reforms did not affect vast masses of the Russian people. In fact, many Western observers of Russia during Peter's reign and shortly thereafter reported that the country was hardly Westernized at all by Peter's reforms. Voltaire emphasized this point in his history of Peter's reign, from which we have taken our seventh passage (the text is translated here by M. F. O. Jenkins).

Our eighth passage is the funeral oration for Peter delivered by Archbishop Theophanes at the Church of Saints Peter and Paul in St. Petersburg on March 10, 1725 (translated by Consett). It reveals the sentiment held by many contemporary Russians, especially those who benefitted from his reforms and shared his vision of transforming Russian into a great power.

Many of the passages selected for this and the following section were written by individuals who were contemporaries of and often participants in the events described. These accounts, consequently, are usually written from a particular perspective, and sometimes display a definite bias mandated or conditioned by social, political, economic or personal preference. One can see this in Johann-Georg Korb, an Austrian Roman Catholic who is critically, even inimically disposed towards Russian Orthodoxy; in Archbishop Theophanes (Feofan) who came as much to praise Peter as to bury him—yet his oration capsulizes Peter's achievements as seen by a favorably-disposed contemporary; and in Voltaire, who compared Russian customs with those of the West, and it may be that this last author's occassional "Russian bias" was mandated as much by a wish to criticize Western customs as by a desire to praise the Russians.

By offering contemporary accounts of persons and events we have run the risk of presenting what others may regard as slanted descriptions. That is *unavoidable. Decades and centuries later, historians still may disagree on interpretation of events. Contemporaries taking part in such events may disagree even more categorically than later day historians. As a result, our collection may lose something in terms of objectivity, but we hope that it compensates for objectivity lost by capturing and presenting a flavor of the pooch described as seen, sensed and experienced by people who actually lived at the time in question and, in many cases, themselves played an active role in shaping the history of the period.*

*Sometimes, mistranslations made by one person are repeated by others. Scholars are not exempt from the practice. Thus, in the passages quoted the title employed by the Russian monarchs is rendered as Tsar "of all the Russians," with the name of the country appearing in the plural form. The Russian text itself-*vseia Rusi-*employs both the adjective "all" and the personal noun "Russia" in the singular (not plural) form, making it clear that the meaning of the phrase was "of all Russia." A source of the mistranslation might have been the use of the somewhat archaic singular form* vseia *of the pronoun "all."*

In order to preserve the flavor of the epoch, archaisms in spelling of quoted texts have been preserved. Specifically, "s" is designated with "f," and capital "J" is designated with capital "F." This may cause the reader some initial difficulty, but with a little practice, and by entering into the spirit of the text, this initial difficulty should be easily overcome (an example of this can be seen on page 21, where "Russians" become "Ruffians").

✤ *Table of Ranks, January 24, 1722*[1]

Military Ranks		Civilian Ranks	Grades
Naval Forces	*Land Forces*		
General-Admiral	Generalissimo FieldMarshal	Chancellor or Active Privy Counselor	I
Admiral	General of Artillery General of Cavalry General of Infantry	Active Privy Counselor	II
Vice Admiral	Lieutenant General	Privy Counselor	III
Rear Admiral	Major General	Active State Counselor	IV
Captain-Commander	Brigadier	State Counselor	V
First Captain	Colonel	Collegial Counselor	VI
Second Captain	Lieutenant Colonel	Court Counselor	VII
Lieutenant-Captain of the Fleet Third Captain of the Artillery	Major	Collegial Assessor	VIII
Lieutenant of the Fleet Lieutenant-Captain of Artillery	Captain or Cavalry Captain	Title Counselor	IX
Lieutenant of Artillery	Staff Captain or Staff Cavalry Captain	Collegial Secretary	X
		Secretary of the Senate	XI
Midshipman	Lieutenant	*Gubernia* Secretary	XII
Artillery Constable	Sublieutenant	Registrar of the Senate	XIII
	Guidon Bearer	Collegial Registrar	XIV

1. Excerpt from *Imperial Russia: A Source Book, 1700–1917,* Second Edition by Basil Dmystryshyn, pp. 17–18, copyright © 1974 by Holt, Rinehart and Winston, Inc., reprinted by permission of the publisher.

Photo: Bronze Horseman Monument of Peter the Great on Decembrist Square (formerly Senate Square) in St. Petersburg.

✤ *Decrees on the Duties of the Senate*[1]

This *ukaz* [decree] should be made known. We have decreed that during our absence administration of the country is to be [in the hands of] the Governing Senate [consisting of the following persons]: Count Musin Pushkin, *gospodin* [Lord] Strezhnev, Prince Peter Golitsyn, Prince Micheal Dolgoruky, *gospodin* Plemiannikov, Prince Gregory Volkonskii, *gospodin* Samarin, *gospodin* Vasili Opukhtin, [and] *gospodin* Melnitskii; Anisim Shchukin [is to act as] the Senate's Chief Secretary. Vasili Ershov is to administer the Moscow Gubernia [administrative unit] and to report [on it] to the Senate; the position of Prince Peter Golitsyn is to go to *gospodin* Kurbatov. The Military *prikaz* [department] is to be replaced by the Military Board [and is to be] attached to the above mentioned Senate.

Each *gubernia* is to send two officials to advise the Senate on judicial and legislative matters . . .

In our absence the Senate is charged by this *ukaz* with the following:

1. To establish a just court, to deprive unjust judges of their offices and of all their property, and to administer the same treatment to all slanderers.
2. To supervise governmental expenditures throughout the country and cancel unnecessary and, above all, useless things.
3. To collect as much money as possible because money is the artery of war.
4. To recruit young noblemen for officer training, especially those who try to evade it; also to select about 1000 educated boyars for the same purpose.
5. To reform letters of exchange and keep these in one place.
6. To take inventory of goods leased to offices or *gubernias*.
7. To farm out the salt trade in an effort to receive some profit [for the state].
8. To organize a good company and assign to it the China trade.
9. To increase trade with Persia and by all possible means to attract in great numbers Armenians [to that trade]. To organize inspectors and inform them of their responsibilities.

---

1. Excerpt from *Imperial Russia: A Source Book, 1700–1917*, Second Edition by Basil Dmystryshyn, pp. 13–14, copyright © 1974 by Holt, Rinehart and Winston, Inc., reprinted by permission of the publisher.

❖ *Letter from Peter to the Holy Synod (August 30, 1722)*[1]

We acquaint you, that from *Aftracan* we went by the Sea to *Terik*, and from *Terik* to *Agracan*, from whence we difpatch'd our Univerfals. And there being landed, we waited a long Time for the Cavalry; which met with inexpreffible Difficulty in their March, for want of Water, and by Reafon of bad Grafs; efpecially the Body that came from *Aftracan*, under the Command of Major General *Cropotoff*, Orders were fent to Brigadier *Viterani* to march to *Andrew's* Village, and plunder it, if not fortify'd as was reported. And whilft he was yet upon his March, and advanc'd near the Place, the Enemy fet upon him in the Road; but by God's Affiftance they were defeated, and their Town taken, which as is faid confifted of 3000d Houfes. Our Men plunder'd and burnt them to Afhes, then return'd to us; as alfo *Cropotoff* at the fame Time came from *Aftracan*. Whom having receiv'd, we proceeded on our March, and came to this Place, all was ftill and quiet in the Road, and the Dageftan (or Mountain) Princes receiv'd us with a Countenance and Appearance of Amity and Kindnefs (but this Friendfhip of theirs was an Expreffion of their Good-will, like that Acknowledgment of the Divinity of Chrift, *What have we to do with thee, Jesus, thou Son of the Living God*). Only as we enter'd the Government of Sultan *Mahmut Outemifboff*, he gave us no Invitation, wherefore we fent three Dons Coffacks, with a Letter to him, on the 19th of *Auguft*, in the Morning; and the fame Day, at 3 a Clock in the Afternoon, the faid Gentleman was pleas'd to attack us unexpectedly (thinking to have taken us unprepar'd) we were very glad of our Gueft (efpecially the Lads that have not heard the Whizz of a Ball) and receiving him, we conducted him with our Horfe, and a third Part of the Foot, to his own Quarters, returning his Vifit; and whilft we were there, we entertain'd him with a Bonefire of his whole Dominion (namely, in one Place, where he refided, 500d Houfes were burnt, befides 6 other Villages on each Side of it). The Prifoners and the Governours our Friends agree in relating, that he had 10000d Men, who were not all his own People, but out of feveral Provinces under his Name; and very near half Foot, 600d of which are reckon'd to be flain, and only 30 taken Prifoners. Our side 5 Dragoons and 7 Coffacks were kill'd; but our Infantry neither got or loft any thing, becaufe the Enemy did not wait their coming up.

Afterwards, as foon as we came near this City, the Naip (or Vice-Governour) of the place met us, and deliver'd up the Key of the Gate.

In Truth, this People receiv'd us with an undiffembled Affection and Zeal, and were as glad of us as if we had deliver'd them from a Siege.

---

1. Reprinted from James Cracraft, ed. *For God and Peter the Great, The Works of Thomas Consett, 1723–1729* (New York, Columbia University Press, 1982), pp. 223–226.

From *Baku* a Letter was fend to us of the fame Import, with that which we had receiv'd from this City before we approach'd it; for which Reafon we alfo defign to fend a Garrifon thither.

And thus, by the Bleffing of God, we have got footing in thefe Borders, with which we Greet you. This March, tho' not far diftant, is yet very troublefome, becaufe of exceffive Heats, and for want of Forage for the Horfe. But to inform you more particularly in what is pafs't I have fubjoin'd a Journal. We fhall alfo write to you Accounts for future Proceedings.

✤ *An Instruction to Russian Students Abroad Studying Navigation*[1]

1. Learn [how to draw] plans and charts and how to use the compass and other naval indicators.
2. [Learn] how to navigate a vessel in battle as well as in a simple maneuver, and learn how to use all appropriate tools and instruments; namely, sails, ropes, and oars, and the like matters, on row boats and other vessels.
3. Discover as much as possible how to put ships to sea during a naval battle. Those who cannot succeed in this effort must diligently ascertain what action should be taken by the vessels that do and those that do not put to sea during such a situation [naval battle]. Obtain from [foreign] naval officers written statements, bearing their signatures and seals, of how adequately you [Russian students] are prepared for [naval] duties.
4. If, upon his return, anyone wishes to receive [from the Tsar] greater favors for himself, he should learn in addition to the above enumerated instructions, how to construct those vessels aboard which he would like to demonstrate his skills.
5. Upon his return to Moscow, every [foreign-trained Russian] should bring with him at his own expense, for which he will later be reimbursed, at least two experienced masters of naval science. They [the returnees] will be assigned soldiers, one soldier per returnee, to teach them [what they have learned abroad]. And if they do not wish to accept soldiers they may teach their acquaintances or their own people. The treasury will pay for transportation and maintenance of soldiers. And if anyone other than soldiers learns [the art of navigation] the treasury will pay 100 rubles for the maintenance of every such individual . . .

Excerpt from *Imperial Russia: A Source Book, 1700–1917,* Second Edition by Basil Dmystryshyn, p. 16, copyright © 1974 by Holt, Rinehart and Winston, Inc., reprinted by permission of the publisher.

The Story of the Ship's-Boat, Which Gave his Majefty the Thought of Building Ships of War[1]

The genuine history of this Boat, and the Occafion his Tfarifh Majefty took from the accidental Sight of it, to fet about the building of a Fleet, ftands in the Preface to the (Morskoi Ouftave or) Sea Regulation: Wherein fome Notice is taken of the Difficulty to reprefent the ancient State of *Ruffia* for want of Hiftories, they having no Account of any Thing till after the Time of Duke *Ruric,* who died in 879. *Cluverius* is quoted for the Relation he gives from *Greek* Hiftorians of *Igor,* Great Duke of *Ruffia,* his croffing the *Euxin* with a Fleet of 15000d Veffels to attack *Conftantinople;* but thefe are agreed to have been only meer Cock-boats, and of no Confequence. Then it is obferv'd, that Duke *Uladimir* was too much engag'd in eftablifhing Religion to regard Navigation; and is blam'd for the Divifion he made of his Country into twelve Dukedoms for the Sake of his twelve Sons; but the Difturbances which this Diftribution had occafion'd, were quieted by the Great Knaze or Prince *Ivan Bafilowich,* who reunited thefe Dukedoms, and reduc'd them again into one Body. This Succefs by Land gave great Umbrage to the maritime Powers, left fuch an enterprizing Prince fhould make any Attempts by Sea; and therefore in a Congrefs at *Lubeck,* the Subjects of Foreigners were forbid to come into *Ruffia* to teach them Navigation, or to build Ships; tho' this feems not to have been his Defign, his whole Time being taken up in making Conquefts by Land. The Death of *Borife Godunoff* concluded the Succeffion in his Line; and then after an Interregnum of fome Years, to the Hiftories of which the Preface refers us; came on the Family of the prefent Tfar PETER the Great; firft, his Grandfather Tfar *Micheal Theodorowitch,* who quell'd the Civil Diffentions of the Country, and guarded againft the Incurfions of the *Tarters,* had yet no Thought of building Ships. Again, his Father Tfar *Alexie Michaelowich,* not only confirm'd the Strength of the Country as his Father left it, but advanc'd upon his Neighbours, and enlarg'd his Territories, and extended his Thoughts alfo towards the Sea. Yet in this he made but a very small Beginning, having only built a little ship call'd the EAGLE, and one Yacht or Galliot in the River *Volga;* and this Defign was totally quafh'd and defeated at *Aftracan,* by a Quarrel amongft the *Hollanders,* that built and had the Care of thefe Veffels, in their Way to the *Cafpian.* The Captain being kill'd, fome fled to *Perfia,* and thence to the

---

1. Reprinted from James Cracraft, ed. *For God and Peter the Great, The Works of Thomas Consett, 1723–1729* (New York, Columbia University Press, 1982), pp. 205–220

Indies; only two of the whole Company, a Surgeon and a Carpenter return'd to *Mofco* to relate the Difappointment. So that Tfar *Peter Alexiewich* truly began and perfected a Fleet. The Story of which is thus related from the 32nd Page, to the end of this Preface.

And here we fee indeed a like Divine Providence, as was obfervable in the Building of the firft Temple of the Lord in *Ferufalem. David* had purpos'd with great Zeal to build a Temple; but God forbid him that Undertaking, and devolv'd it on his Son *Solomon:* And fo with us, Ship-building defign'd and begun by Tfar *Alexie,* the incomprehenfible Counfel of God did not permit to be perfected by him; but determin'd that his Son PETER the Firft fhould be Author of this Work. And tho' the Father's Intention was not accomplifh'd, yet that redounds to his eternal Honour; becaufe it fhews us abundantly the enterprizing Spirit of that Monarch; and from that Beginning, as from a good Seed, the prefent Naval Works are fprung up.

We come now to the Fpecial Narration of our Happinefs. And mark Reader, in what an ample Manner, and by what a wonderful Providence this has commenc'd and grown to the greateft Maturity.

The now reigning, and our moft gracious Monarch, in the Beginning of his Reign, whilft he was yet a Youth, gave Proof of his great Soul, and how fit he was for fuch an Empire. He was excited by his own nartual Genius to improve himfelf in every commendable Practice, and by an inflexible Inclination to Sciencc and Action. The Defign and Beginning of this great Work of building a Fleet, did not take its Rife From an Obfervation and Sight of large and wonderful Arfenals and Navies, but from fo fmall an Accident, as could fcarce be thought of, as follows.

It happen'd that his Majefty was in the Flax-yard at *Ifmaeloff,* and walking by the Magazines, where fome Remains of the Houfhold Furniture of *Niketa Ivanowich Romanoff,* his Great Uncle were laid, he efpy'd amongft other Things a fmall foreign Veffel, and his native Curiofity not fuffering him to pafs it by without an Enquiry, he prefently ask'd *Francis Timerman* (who then liv'd with him, and taught him Geometry and Fortification) what was that? He told him it was an *Englifh* Boat. The Sovereign again ask'd, Where did they make Ufe of it? *Timerman* anfwer'd, It was us'd by Ships to bring and carry Goods. Then again, his Majefty ask'd, In what is it preferable to our Veffels (for he obferv'd it to be built in a Fafhion better and ftronger than ours) *Timerman* anfwer'd, that it goes with a Sail, with a Wind, or againft it; which Word made him greatly Wonder; and as tho' not credible, rais'd his Curiofity to fee a Proof of it. The Monarch ask'd the faid *Timerman,* was there fuch a Man as could refit the Veffel, and fhew it to go fo? And hearing that there was one, being overjoy'd he requir'd them to find him out. Then *Timerman* fought out the abovefaid Carpenter *Carftens Brand* (who was fent for by his Father from *Holland* to build Ships in the *Cafpian,* as is above related.)

Then did the Seed of Tfar *Alexie Michaelowitch* begin to fprout. *Carftens Brand* a long Time defpairing of Employ in his own Way, had hitherto fubfifted himfelf by Joyner's Work; and contrary to his Expectation, being call'd to work in his firft Trade, he very willingly repair'd the Boat, made the Maft and Sails, and fail'd up and down the River *Taufe* in his Majefty's Sight, which was yet a greater Wonder to his Majefty, and exceedingly pleas'd him.

And who at that Time could imagine this Divertifement of his Majefty wou'd ever have been improv'd to greater Purpofes, and not have been laid afide as an Entertainment of his Youth? But this Monarch was fo particularly remarkable in all he did, that the very Paftimes of his Childhood are efteem'd, as Tranfactions momentous and weighty, and appear worthy to be recorded in Hiftory. He purfu'd fuch Diverfions in his Childhood as lead him, and many other great Perfonages before him, to future great Exploits. His Pleafures were to build Forts moated round, to draw up Battalions as a real Engagement with an Enemy, offenfive and detenfive. And fo, the faid Boat did not only ferve for Play and Paftime, but gave Occafion for his building a great Fleet, as we now fee with juft Admiration.

But to return to the Beginning of this Story, his Majefty was not content to fee the Sailing of the Boat, but he coveted himfelf to go in her, and fteer her. And becaufe he obferv'd the Boat not to anfwer her Helm, but often to ftrike againft the Bank, he ask'd the abovefaid *Carftens Brand* the Reafons of it; he anfwer'd, becaufe the Water was narrow, and fhe had not fufficient Way. Then his Majefty order'd the Boat to be carry'd into a Water call'd the *Profian Pond;* but this was nothing better, and his Defire was fo inflam'd, that it hourly encreas'd, and he refolv'd to carry it into a larger Water, and the Lake of *Pereflave* was mention'd to him as neareft. He wifhed to fly thither, but fee what interven'd to retard this Journey!

His Mother, of immortal Memory, the moft Auguft Tfarene of *Ruffia*, being heartily folicitous for the Safety of her Son, endeavour'd to diffuade and divert him from it; yet with a Deference and Refpect to his Sovereign Dignity: On his Part, he fo comported himfelf to the Will of his Mother, as if regardlefs of his own Power and Majefty.

Here was the Difficulty; to defift from his intended Journey towards the Lake, his ftrong Bent of Mind that Way would not permit, and yet to proceed without his Mother's Approbation, his filial Affection forbid him; and the Scruple was about her Majefty's Confent, in an Undertaking, at leaft in Opinion, dangerous. However, his eager Defire to effect his Purpofe, made him very thoughtful how to bring it about, under the Pretext of performing a Vow in *Trinity* Monaftery, he prevail'd with his Auguft Mother for an Opportunity of making this Journey; hence it is manifeft, with what an ardent Zeal, for the common Good, God infpir'd this Monarch.

After his Majefty had taken a full View of the Extent of this Lake, he then inftantly and openly entreated his Mother to build there a Houfe and Veffels. And fo the abovefaid *Carftens Brand,* build fmall Frigates and Three Yachts, wherein his Majefty diverted himfelf a few Years. But afterwards he thought this too fmall a Water, and defign'd to go to the *Lake Cubins*, which is large and extenfive, but not deep enough. Then he fix'd his Refolution to Vifit a Water large as his Defire, and that was the Sea itfelf; but Motherly Care again obftructed this Defign, which often reprefented this as a Voyage dangerous and troublefome; but fuch was the Impulfe of the Son's Spirit, that it could not be reftrain'd nor diverted, and fhe faw him immutably refolv'd, notwithftanding all the Diffuafion fhe had us'd.

Therefore, in 1694, his Majefty vifited *Arch-Angel*, and from thence in his own Yacht, call'd the St. PETER, he fail'd to *Ponoia*, in Company with *Englifh* and *Hollands* Merchant Ships, under Convoy of one *Hollands* Man of War, Commanded by Captain *Folle Folfon*.

His Majefty was much delighted with his Voyage, fo much at large, but did not ftop here, and therefore bent his Thoughts wholly towards building a Fleet. And when in his Invafion of the *Tartars*, he had laid Siege to *Afoph*, and happily taken it, he then in Profecution of his Purpofe, which was unchangable, thought not long about it, but put it fpeedily in Execution. A fit Place for building Ships was found in the River *Verenez*, by a City of the fame Name. Mafters were fent for from *Holland*, and in 1696, a new Work was begun in *Ruffia*, the building of great and noble Ships, Gallies, and other Veffels, and to make it lafting in *Ruffia*, he contriv'd to bring the Art itfelf into his own Nation; and for that End fent great Numbers of his own Nobility and Gentry into *Holland*, and other Dominions, to learn Ship-building and Navigation.

And what is moft wonderful, as tho' this Monarch was afham'd to be out-done by his Subjects in this Art, he made a Tour to *Holland* himfelf, and at *Amfterdam*, in the Woodyard call'd the *Oftend*-Wharf, he wrought with other Volunties in the Ships, and in a little Time made that Proficiency as to parfs for a good Carpenter. After this, he defir'd *John Pool*, Mafter of the Yard, to inftruct him in the Proportions of a Ship, which he learn'd in four Days. But becaufe in *Holland*, this Art was not taught perfectly, in the Mathematical Way, but only fome Principles of it, and the reft muft be acquir'd by long Practice and Experience; and the abovefaid Mafter told him, that they could not demonftrate this in Lines. It gave him great Uneafinefs, that he had taken fo long a Journey for that Purpofe, and had fail'd of his End, fo much defir'd. A few Days after, it happen'd that his Majefty was at the Houfe of *John Theefing* a Merchant, where he fate in Company very penfive for the abovefaid Reafon; but when in the Courfe of Converfation, he was ask'd the Caufe of his Melancholly, he then declar'd the above Reafon for it.

An *Englifh* Man in the Company who heard this, told him, that with us in *England*, this Kind of Structure was in the fame Perfection as other Arts and Sciences, and might be learn'd in a fhort Time. His Majefty was glad to hear this, and hereupon went in all hafte to *England*, and there, in four Months Time, finifh'd his Learning; and at his Return, brought over with him two Mafter Ship-builders, *John Dean* and *Jofeph Noy*.

And now it appears to have been an Incident, not a little remarkable, fince we have a compleat Fleet in *Ruffia,* and the *Ruffian* Monarch himfelf was a Mafter Ship-builder; as he prov'd in Fact, by appointing another Place for building Ships in this Royal City, which he has founded. What a Multitude of great Ships, and Gallies, and other Veffels of every Kind, are here built regularly and beautifully, we have no Occafion to relate; we all See, Rejoice and Wonder. And becaufe a Fleet, to enable it to fucceed in Expeditions and Engagements, requires fome Form of Regulation, or a Rule, without which, Winds or Sailors are ufelefs, the moft wife Monarch fet himfelf to this Work, and partly from his own Judgement, and partly out of the Regulations of Foreigners, he collected the excellent Rules in this Book. And thus he has as it were, breath'd a living Soul into his own material Creation; and thence we have feen by the Bleffing of God thofe happy Succeffes in every Part of the *Baltick;* where he made Prize of a great many Ships of Enemies; with unufual Succefs took the *Swedes* Rear-Admiral and his Squadron, and fubdu'd the Great Kingdom of *Finland,* which by Land was never to come at, by Reafon of the Difficulty of the Roads to it. And in 1719 laft pafs'd, by a Defcent on *Sweden* itfelf, he gave them fuch a Defeat as concluded in our Advantage and Triumph.

See now, kind Reader, how merciful the moft gracious God has been, and how wonderful his Providence manifefted to us! In old Time as low as the moft ancient Hiftories go, *Ruffia* had no Fleet; tho' this was always poffible, had there been any Thought or Care to have One; afterwards adverfe Times arofe wherein it was impracticable fo much as to think about it. But in our Days this glorious Work, fcarce before heard of by us, having taken its Beginning and Rife from fo fmall an Occafion, is grown to the greateft Perfection by the Vigilancy, Diligence, and indefatigable Application and Induftry of this moft wife Monarch; and this, in fuch a ftrange and wonderful Manner, as a long and tedious War has not oblig'd him to intermitt, nor many other Cares about Civil and Military, have given the leaft Interruption to it.

The Story being thus told in the Preface, as above, can want no Confirmation; yet to fhew farther, in an Inftance very remarkable, the Paffion his Majesty had for this little Boat, I prefume to add the laft Token of his Regard for it; whereby he feem'd defirous to perpetuate the Remembrance of it, as the firft Occafion of his Naval Proceedings and Exploits.

This very Boat was brought from *Mofco* to St. *Petersburgh* in 1723, repair'd and beautify'd, in order to make her laft, and moft glorious Appearance, on the 12th of *Auguft,* which I fhall give a fhort Account of, as I had an Opportunity of feeing the Tranfaction.

In *June* Month, this Year, his Majefty fail'd to *Revel* with his Fleet, and return'd to *Croonftadt* in the Beginning of *Auguft;* at which time a great Number of Yatchts and Buyers (faid to be 200d) and one Galliot, were order'd to meet him there, and to attend on the famous Little Boat, above defcrib'd.

After this little Fleet was arriv'd within half a league of that Place with their Charge, they had Orders to caft Anchor, till the nine Flags in fo many

Pinnaces, came up to pay their Refpects to the Mother of their great Fleet. A fmall Parent indeed of fo large a Progeny! At the Return of the Flags the Yachts, & c. weigh'd Anchor and went into Haven, fave the Galliot, which boar the venerable Matron that lay off at Sea, till the Day of the grand Solemnity, when fhe was receiv'd with uncommon Ceremony. For the Great Prince of fecond Time made her a Vifit with the Flags alone, launch'd her, and grac'd her with his Imperial Standard, his own Perfon fteering, the great Admiral, and two other Admirals rowing, with the Surveyor of the Navy *Ivan Michaelowitch Golovin*. At her launching the Great Admiral General fir'd feven Guns as a fignal to the whole Fleet, confifting of twenty two Men of War of the Line, to fire at once: Then away fhe came, and as fhe row'd by each Ship, was faluted by all the Canon.

After fhe had pafs'd the whole Fleet, and row'd into the Haven, the dutiful children paid their laft Compliment to their Mother with one general Salute of their Canon. Then came on Dinner-time, and in the Evening the court and Flag-Officers rendezvouz'd on the Edges of the Haven, and clos'd the Scene with Merriment, and Drink enough.

A few Days after, the Boat was brought back to *Petersburgh,* and laid up in the Caftle, where fhe is to be taken the greateft Care of.

✢ *Baptism*[1]

The Ruffians deny that perfons are truly baptifed who are regenerated, according to the Roman rite by the mere fprinkling with water in the name of the moft Holy Trinity; but contend, with moft obftinate fuperftition, that baptifm fhould be performed by immerfion; that the old man muft be drowned (*suffocari*) in the water, which is to be done by immerfion, and not by afperfion. Infifting pertinacioufly upon this error, they admit reiteration of baptifm, and baptife anew, either by immerfion or, as the present ufage is, by pouring water over the whole body from head to foot, any perfons, no matter what religion they may have previoufly belonged to, who embrace the Ruffian fchifm, either of their own free will, or, as is generally the cafe, upon compulfion. And becaufe there are three perfons in the Godhead, fo they require a triple immerfion.

1. Reprinted from Johann-Georg Korb (The Count MacDonnell, trans), *Diary of an Austrian Secretary of Legation at the Court of Peter the Great* (London, Frank Cass and Company, LTD, 1863), pp. 174–184, 206–216.

Sacrifice

They celebrate according to the Greek rite; they ufe leavened bread and red wine; they diftribute the confecrated bread and wine together out of the chalice with a fpoon. Though they commonly make ufe of red wine for the facrifice, yet if it is not to be had, they do not deny that white wine may be confecrated.

They hardly or with difficulty permit ftrangers or thofe that are not of their religion to enter their churches. For Catholics, however, they are lefs particular than for Lutherans and Calvinifts. Perhaps becaufe they are aware that we venerate the images and relics of faints, and that the others fpurn them.

Of Images

They venerate only painted images, and not fuch as are fculptured or wrought in any other manner; for they will have it that it is forbidden by the commandment of God in the Decalogue to adore any graven thing, which precept, however, in the way in which *adoration* ought to be underftood, equally prohibits the painted and the graven.

Sermons

The Ruffians, up to the prefent, have always condemned the functions of preachers, faying that profeffed preachers affect rather a ufelefs elegance of language than earneftnefs in proclaiming the word of God. Yet in the prefent age the practice of expounding the Gofpel has met with the approval of the Ruffians. For there are even fome to be found among them who, confident of their own learning, are not content with merely reading the Gofpel or holy Scripture aloud in the church (which was the old fafhion), but prefer a polifhed and rhetorically laboured difcourfe of their own compofition.

Their Veneration for the Mother of God

They venerate the Mother of God with the moft devout piety, and they hold it to be right and ufeful to reverence God's faints. They hold Saint Nicholas in principal veneration and honour, on which account they celebrate that faint's feftival twice a year.

Monasteries

They have monks and nuns who, in aufterity of life, in frequency of fafts, in rigour and poverty, exceed the difcipline of our religious in feverity, but not in piety. For in the feafon of their fafts they macerate the flefh to fuch a degree that it is held finful to give even medicine to the fick; but when the time of the faft is over, they make ufe of every licenfe; and, more like debauchees than monks, they are rampant drunk in the public places; and, devoid of all fhame, they are often found in lafcivioufnefs in the open ftreets. They wear a long black gown, with a cowl at the neck. They are all meanly dreffed, except thofe that bear the higher offices in the monafteries, who are more expenfively clothed. They alfo make the three vows of chaftity, poverty, and obedience. They are not imbued with letters. Sometimes Poles, deferting to their fchifm, are mixed up in thefe monafteries. Such a one I found in the monaftery called Jerufalem, which lies fix miles diftant from Mofcow.

❖

Festival Days

There are almoft as many feftivals in Ruffia as there are days in the year: but the feftivals alternate between the different quarters of the city; fo that while one quarter is keeping holiday, the other is working. But the major feftivals of the Nativity, the Refurrection, the Afcenfion, &c., they all keep holy together, which they indicate by a continual and annoying jangling of a bell. If bell-ringing and the outward piety of making the fign of the crofs be fufficient to conftitute true Chriftian devotion, Mufcovy, at this prefent day, can prefent us with multitudes of excedingly Chriftian folk. On feftival days they only reft from labour in the forenoon; at a very early hour in the morning, generally before daybreak, they get through their facred functions in the dark, and the day itfelf they confecrate, if not to work, at leaft to debauchery: fo that one muft always be in fear of a conflagration as often as the Ruffians celebrate a feftival, or, as they call it, *brafnick*.

❖

Burial

They ufe a number of ceremonies in the burial of their dead. They bring fuperftitious and profane women for thofe occafions, who follow the funeral with mercenary fobs. In the coffin they hide letters of recommendation to Saint Nicholas, whom they believe to be the doorkeeper of heaven: and in thefe letters the Patriarch affeverates that the deceafed led the life of a Chriftian, and at length died with praifeworthy conftancy in the orthodox Ruffian faith. When the corpfe is laid in the grave, a pope, after a fhort fermon upon the neceffity of dying, throws in the firft burial earth. Befides the prayers for the dead after the bodies have been committed to the ground, they have women at the grave, who fet up a loud howling and wail, and afk the deceafed, with mighty vociferation, after the manner of the pagans, *"Why did they die?* Why did they fo foon defert their dear fweet wives?— their darling offspring? What did they want for? Meat? Drink?"* Finally, they place upon the grave various defcriptions of food, to be divided among the poor who are in the habit of gathering in crowds there. This they often repeat during the year, out of affection and charity towards the departed.

Of Female Luxury

The women of Mufcovy are graceful in figure, and fair and comely of feature: but fpoil their beauty with needlefs fhams. Their fhapes, unimprifoned by ftays, are free to grow as nature bids, and are not of fo neat and trim figure as thofe of other Europeans. They wear chemifes interwoven with gold all through, the fleeves of which are plaited up in a marvellous way, being eight and fometimes ten ells in length, and their pretty concatenation of little plaits extends down to the hands, and is confined with handfome and coftly bracelets. Their outer garments refemble thofe of Eaftern women: they wear a cloak over their tunic. They often drefs in handfome filks and furs, and earrings and rings are in general fafhion among them. Matrons and widows cover the head with furs of price: maidens only wear a rich band round their forehead and go bareheaded, wiht their locks floating upon their fhoulders, and arranged with great elegance in artificial knots.

Thofe of any dignity or honourable condition are not urged to be prefent at banquets, nor do they even fit at the ordinary table of their hufbands. They may be feen, neverthelefs, at prefent when they go to church or drive out to vifit their friends; for there has been a great relaxation of the jealous old rule which required women only to go out in carriages fo clofed up, that the very ufe of eyefight was denied to thefe creatures made bond-flaves to a mafter. Moreover, they hold it among the greateft honours that can be paid if a hufband admits his gueft to fee his wife or daughters, who prefent a glafs of brandy, and expect a kifs from the favoured guefts; and, according to the manner of this people, duly propitiated with this, they withdraw in filence, as they came. They exercife no authority in their houfeholds. When the mafter is abfent from home, the fervants have full charge of the management of the affairs of the houfe, according to their honefty or caprice, without afking or acquainting the wife about anything. But the more wealthy maintain great crowds of handmaidens, who do fcarcely any work, except what trifling things the wife may require of them; meantime, they are kept fhut up in the houfe, and fpin and weave linen. With fuch a lazy life one cannot blame the cuftom which condemned the poor creatures to fuch frequent ufe of the bath, fo that their idlenefs may be at leaft varied from time to time with another defcription of floth.

Whenever the wife of a man of the higher claffes is delivered of a child, they fignify it without delay to the *employés* and tradefmen, with rather a beggarly kind of civility. Thofe who dread the hufband's power, or are ambitious of his patronage, on receiving notice of the new birth, come to offer their congratulations in return; and giving a kifs to the mother, they prefent fome offering as a token for the new-borne babe. They had better beware not to give lefs than a gold piece, for that would be a kind of vilipending; but everybody is free to be more generous in his gift. He that is found to be the moft liberal will be deemed the beft friend. What the poet fang of the populace, I apply with greater juftice to the Mufcovites—the Mufcovite tefts friendfhip by its utility. It is a fable that they value the affection of their hufbands for they by the amount of blows they receive from them; for they know how to diftinguifh between ferocious and gentle characters better than words can tell. If any perfon of weight were to make a beginning of abandoning the old ufage, they would certainly ftruggle from beneath that moft vile bondage in which they are held towards their hufbands.

The Mufcovites hold it finful to marry a fourth wife; in confequence of which the third is in general treated famoufly, although her two predeceffors are treated like bond-flaves; for the thoughts of a new wife, and their inordinate defires, induce them to wifh for their fpeedy death, and render the charms of the firft loathfome, perhaps even within the brief fpace of a year. It is quite a proverb, that a pope may have one and a layman a third wife. Becaufe when thefe die it is unlawful for them to marry again, and the Mufcovites treat thefe with true marital affection, as they never can expect to marry again when thefe die. Neverthelefs, fome of the more powerful extort a difpenfation from the Patriarch to marry a fourth time; and the Patriarch, even though he does not refufe it, ftill blames them as facrilegious nuptials, that are null in virtue of the immutable authority of the prohibitive law. The Don Coffacks have another cuftom. They may repudiate women *ad libitum*, provided it be in the circle of the whole community, which affembly they call a Krug. In preference of the *Atamann* and the entire community the man leads his wife into the middle of the circle, and proclaims that fhe pleafes him no longer; this faid, he twirls his wife round about, and letting her go, pronounces her free from his marital authority. The byftander who takes hold of the difcarded woman is compelled to keep her as a wife, and protect and maintain her until the next affembly day. Still the laws of thefe barbarians have eftablifhed rules for repudiations; fo that they are not valid, except in circle and with the whole community as witneffes.

Thefe cuftoms differ but flightly from that whereby men of free condition, in Turkey, join in wedlock with their female flaves before the Woivode: an affociation of man and woman which is the next thing to concubinage: for the bond may be diffolved at the man's caprice. One intending to take a wife in this way goes before the Woivode and acquaints him with his intention. The latter, when about to join thefe perfons, afks them for a belt (*cingulum*) and a little chaplet of flowers (*ftrophiolum*) from the woman, and the propofal being made to the woman, and a certain dowry promifed,— for example, fifty imperials,—he gives the belt to the woman and the chaplet to the man, then takes note of the date and what takes place, and writes down fome particular marks of the parties. When the man becomes tired of the woman, he has to call again on the Woivode, before whom the affair muft be laid again; and he, for a fee of two or three imperials—having firft exacted the promifed dowry for the woman—demands back from the man the chaplet he formerly received, and the belt from the woman, and, returning the belt to the man and the chaplet to the woman, he diffolves the marriage, and pronounces both free.

✤ *Voltaire's View of Peter's Russia*[1]

Thanks to the poll-tax register and the census figure of merchants, artisans, and male peasants, I am in a position to vouch for the fact that modern Russia has at least twenty-four million inhabitants. The majority of these twenty-four million are serfs like those found in Poland, in several German states, and formerly in almost all of Europe. In Russia and Poland the wealth of a nobleman or a churchman is reckoned not according to his income, but by the number of his slaves.

Here are the figures of the 1747 census of males paying the poll tax.

Merchants	198,000
Workmen	16,500

1. Reprinted by permission of the publishers from M. F. O. Jenkins (trans.), *Russian Under Peter the Great*, by Voltaire (Cranbury, N.J., Associated University Presses, Inc., 1983), pp. 57–61, 81–85.

Peasants affiliated with the merchants and workmen	1,950
Peasants called *odnodvortsy* who contribute to the support of the militia	430,220
Others who do not contribute to it	26,080
Workers in various trades, and of unknown parentage	1,000
Others who are not affiliated with the trade guilds	4,700
Peasants immediately dependent upon the crown, approximately	555,000
Workers in the imperial mines, Christians as well as Muslims and pagans	64,000
Other crown peasants working in privately owned mines and factories	24,200
Recent converts to the Orthodox Church	57,000
Pagan Tartars and Ostiaks	241,000
Mourses, Tartars, Mordvinians, and others, either heathen or Orthodox, employed as laborers fo the Admiralty	7,800
Taxpaying Tartars, known as *tepteris* and *bobilitz,* etc	28,900
Serfs belonging to several merchants and other privileged persons who, without being landowners, are permitted to own slaves	9,100
Land serfs intended for the service of the court	418,000
Land serfs belonging to His Majesty in his own right, independently of the rights of the crown	60,500
Land serfs confiscated by the crown	13,600
Noblemen's serfs	3,550,000
Serfs belonging to the Assembly of the Clergy and paying its expenses	37,500
Bishops' serfs	116,400
Serfs belonging to the monasteries, whose numbers were greatly reduced by Peter	721,500
Serfs belonging to cathedral and parish churches	23,700
Peasants employed as laborers for the Admiralty, or other public works, approximately	4,000
Workers in privately owned mines and factories	16,000
Land serfs given to the principal manufacturers	14,500
Workers in the imperial mines	3,000
Bastards brought up by priests	40
Sectarians known as Raskolniki	2,200
TOTAL	6,646,390

In round numbers, that is six million six hundred and forty thousand males paying the poll tax. Male children and old men are included in this enumeration, but women and girls are not, and neither are boys born between one survey and the next. Simply triple the number of taxable heads, include the women and girls, and you will find nearly twenty million souls.

To this total must be added the military, amounting to three hundred and fifty thousand men. Throughout the empire, neither the aristocracy nor the clergy, who number two hundred thousand, are subjects to the poll tax. All foreigners in the empire are exempt, regardless of profession and nationality. The inhabitants of conquered provinces, namely Livonia, Estonia, Ingria, Carelia, and a part of Finland, the Ukrainians and the Cossacks, the Kalmucks and other Tartars, the Samoyeds, Laplanders, Ostiaks, and all the idolatrous tribes of Siberia—a country larger than China—are not included in the census.

According to this calculation, the total population of Russia could not possibly have amounted to less than twenty-four million in 1759, when these records, taken from the imperial achieves, were sent to me. By this count, there are eight persons per square mile. The British ambassador whom I mentioned earlier allows only five persons per square mile, but doubtless he did not have access to records as faithful as those which have been graciously imparted to myself.

The territory of Russia is therefore—*mutatis mutandis*—exactly five times less densely populated than Spain, yet it has nearly four times as many inhabitants. It is almost as populous as France and Germany, but in relation to its immense area the number of people is thirty times fewer.

There is an important comment to be made concerning this enumeration, which is that out of six million six hundred and forty thousand taxpayers, about nine hundred thousand are found to belong to the Russian clergy, not counting either the clergy of the conquered territories or that of the Ukraine and Siberia.

Thus, out of every seven taxable persons, one belongs to the clergy; but despite their one seventh, the clerics are far from enjoying the seventh part of the state's revenues (as is the case in so many other kingdoms, where they possess at least one seventh of all the wealth), for their peasants pay poll tax to the sovereign, and one must make a sizable allowance for the remaining revenues of the Russian crown, in which the clergy does not share.

This assessment differs widely from that made by every other writer on Russia. Foreign envoys who have sent reports to their sovereigns have all been mistaken in this regard. One must scrutinize the imperial archives.

It is highly probable that Russia was once much more populous than it is today, in the period when smallpox, which came from the heart of Arabia, and the other pox, which originated in America, had not yet wrought havoc in the areas where they have since become entrenched. These twin scourges, a greater cause of depopulation than warfare, are due to Mohammed and Christopher Columbus, respectively. The plague, indigenous to Africa, rarely approached the countries of the north. And lastly, since the northern peoples—from the Samaritans to the Tartars beyond the Great Wall of China— have flooded into every part of the world, this ancient seedbed of mankind must have dwindled sadly.

In all this vast expanse of territory, there are estimated to be some seven thousand four hundred monks and five thousand six hundred nuns, despite Peter the Great's endeavors to reduce their numbers, an effort worthy of a lawgiver in an empire where what is principally lacking is people. These thirteen thousand cloistered and—so far as the state is concerned—wasted persons possessed, as the reader will have noted, seven hundred and twenty thousand serfs to cultivate their lands, which is obviously far too many. This abuse, so widespread and detrimental to so many states, was finally ended by the empress Catherine II, who boldly avenged both nature and religion by depriving the secular and regular clergy of a detestable form of wealth. She reimbursed them from the public purse and tried to compel them to be useful, while at the same time preventing them from being dangerous.

I find from the imperial budget of 1725 that, including the tribute paid by the Tartars and all the taxes and duties levied in cash, the total amounted to thirteen million rubles, the equivalent of sixty-five million francs, excluding tributes paid in kind. This paltry sum was then sufficient to maintain three hundred and thirty-nine thousand five hundred soldiers and sailors. The revenues have since increased, and so have the numbers of troops.

In Russia, customs, clothes, and manners had always resembled those of Asia rather than of Christian Europe. Such was the time-honored practice of receiving the people's tributes in the form of produce, of defraying ambassadors' expenses en route and during their period of residence, and that of never appearing in church or before the throne while wearing a sword. This is an oriental practice contrary to our own ridiculous and barbarous custom of conversing with God, kings, our friends, and women with a long offensive weapon trailing at our heels. On ceremonial occasions, the long robe seemed more stately than the shorter garments of Western Europe. A fur-lined tunic with a long gown adorned with precious stones, on solemn occasions, and those lofty turbans which make one taller were more imposing to the eye than perukes and tight-fitting jackets, and more suited to cold climates; but this costume, worn by all peoples in ancient times, seems less appropriate for war and less convenient for work. Nearly all their other usages were uncouth, yet we must not imagine that their manners were as barbarous as many writers say they were. Albert Krants speaks of a czar who had an Italian ambassador's hat nailed to his head because he did not remove it during his speech to the throne. Others attribute this misadventure to a Tartar, and last of all the tale have been told about a French ambassador.

Peter the Great was very tall, relaxed and well-proportioned, with a noble countenance, animated eyes, and a robust constitution fit for any exercise or any labor. He was level-headed, which is the basis for all true talents, and this soundness had a dash of restlessness, which induced him to try everything and achieve everything. His upbringing was quite unworthy of his brilliance; it had been to Princess Sophia's particular advantage to keep him ignorant and to abandon him to the excesses that his youth, idleness, tradition, and rank made only too permissible. However, he had recently married (June, 1689) and had taken to wife, like all other czars, one of his own subjects, the daughter of one Colonel Lopukhin. But as he was a young man and had for some time enjoyed no other royal prerogative save that of indulging in his amusements, the grave responsibilities of marriage did not sufficiently restrain him. The pleasures of the table shared with some foreigners attracted to Moscow by Prime Minister Golitsyn did not herald the fact that Peter would one day become a reformer. Meanwhile, in spite of bad examples and even in spite of his diversions, he applied himself to the military and political arts. It should already have been possible to discern in him the potential great man.

It was even less to be expected that a prince who was overcome with involuntary dread, reaching the point of cold sweats and convulsions, when he had to cross a stream was one day to become the finest seaman of the north. He began to curb nature by throwing himself into the water despite his loathing for this element; his aversion even turned into a dominant preference.

The ignorance in which he had been raised made him blush. Virtually unaided by teachers, he taught himself enough German and Dutch to speak and write intelligibly in both languages. For him, the Germans and Dutch were the most cultivated of peoples, since the former were already practicing in Moscow some of the crafts he wanted to nurture in his empire, and the latter excelled in seamanship, which he regarded as the most indispensable of arts.

Such were his inclinations, notwithstanding the propensities of his youth. However, he had to be constantly on his guard against factions, to check the tempestuous Streltsi, and to sustain an almost unceasing war against the Crimean Tartars. This war ended in 1689 with a short-lived truce.

In the meantime, Peter strengthened his resolve to summon the arts to his native land.

His father, Alexei, had already held the same views, but neither time nor fortune had been in his favor. He passed on his own genius to his son, only more highly developed, more vigorous, and more persistent in the face of obstacles.

At great expense, Alexei had sent for the Dutch shipwright and sea captain Bothler, together with carpenters and sailors, who built a large frigate and a yacht on the Volga. These vessels sailed downstream to Astrakhan. Alexei's intent was to use them, and other ships yet to be constructed, to trade advantageously with Persia across the Caspian Sea. Just then the rebellion of Stenka Razin broke out. The rebel destroyed the two vessels, which he should have preserved in his own interest. He murdered the captain, but the rest of the crew escaped to Persia, and from there reached the territory of the Dutch East India Company. One master carpenter—a good shipbuilder—stayed behind in Russia, where his presence was long overlooked. One day Peter, while taking a stroll at Izmailov, one of his grandfather's country houses, noticed among some other curiosities a small English longboat which had been completely abandoned. He asked his German mathematics teacher, Timmermann, why this little craft was of an entirely different construction from those he had seen on the Moskva. Timmermann replied that it was designed to be both sailed and rowed. The young ruler wanted to try it out there and then, but it had to be refitted and rerigged. They found the shipbuilder Brandt, of whom we have spoken above, living in retirement in Moscow. He overhauled the longboat and sailed it on the Yauza River, which washes the outlaying parts of the city.

Peter had his longboat taken to a large lake near the Troitsa Monastery. He had Brandt build him two frigates and three yachts, which he himself piloted. Eventually, in 1694, he went to Archangel, where, having had a small ship built by the aforementioned Brandt, he set sail on the White Sea, which no czar before him had ever laid eyes on. He was escorted by a Dutch man-of-war commanded by Captain Jolson, and followed by every merchantman berthed at Archangel. He was already learning seamanship, which, despite the alacrity of his courtiers to imitate their sovereign, he alone mastered.

It was no less difficult to train devoted and disciplined soldiers than it was to procure a navy. His first nautical attempts on a lake, before his voyage from Archangel, seemed the mere childhood amusements of a man of genius, and his earliest efforts to train troops also appeared to be no more than a game. This occurred during Sophia's regency, and had anyone suspected that the game was in earnest, it might well have cost Peter his life.

He put his trust in a foreigner, the celebrated Lefort, a member of an ancient Piedmontese noble house which, nearly two centuries before, had removed to Geneva, where it occupied the highest offices. His family wanted to make him a man of business, since that alone is responsible for the importance of Geneva, once famous for nothing but controversy.

Being temperamentally inclined toward higher matters, Lefort left home at the age of fourteen and spent four months as a cadet in the citadel of Marseilles. From there he went to Holland, where he served some time as a volunteer; he was wounded at the siege of Grave-sur-la-Meuse, a quite strongly fortified town which the prince of Orange, later king of England, recaptured from Louis XIV in 1674. After that, seeking advancement wherever his hopes guided him, in 1675 he embarked with a German colonel named Verstein, who had been commissioned by Peter's father, Czar Alexei, to raise some troops in the Netherlands and bring them to the port of Archangel. But when they arrived, after enduring all the perils of the sea, Czar Alexei was no longer living; the government had changed. Russia was in a turmoil, and for a long while the governor of Archangel left Verstein, Lefort, and all their company in the most abject poverty and threatened to send them into the wilds of Siberia. Everyone got away as best he might. Lefort, completely destitute, went to Moscow and presented himself to the Danish Resident, named Van Horn, who made him his secretary. He learned Russian, and shortly thereafter contrived to be presented to Czar Peter, whose elder brother Ivan was not the man for Lefort. Peter took a fancy to him, and, to begin with, gave him the command of an infantry company. Lefort had scarcely any military experience; he was no scholar and had not studied any profession thoroughly. However, he had seen much and seen well; his affinity with the czar was due to his owing everything to the latter's genius. Furthermore, he spoke Dutch and German, which Peter was learning as the languages of two nations that might well serve his designs. Peter liked everything about Lefort, who attached himself to the czar. His position as favorite originated because he was amusing, and was confirmed through his ability. He was privy to the most perilous enterprise that a czar could conceive, namely, preparing himself for the day when he could with impunity smash the mutinous and barbarous Streltsi militia. The great Sultan, or Padishah, Osman's attempt to reform the Janissaries had cost him his life. Despite his youth, Peter went to work more skillfully than Osman had done. To start with, he created a company of fifty of his youngest domestics at his country house at Preobrazhenskoe. A few boyars' sons were chosen to act as officers, but, in order to teach these boyars the chain of command, of which they knew nothing, he made them rise through all the ranks. He personally set the example, serving first as drummerboy, then private, sergeant, and lieutenant in the company. Nothing was more extraordinary nor more salutary. The Russians had always waged war as we used to ourselves during the feudal epoch, when inexperienced noblemen used to lead undisciplined and ill-armed vassals into battle: a barbarous system good enough against similar armies but powerless in the face of regular troops.

This company, Peter's own creation, soon had many effectives, and later became the regiment of Preobrazhensky Guards. A second company, formed on the same model, became the regiment of Semyonovsky Guards.

There already existed one reliable regiment of five thousand men. This had been raised by General Gordon, a Scotsman, and consisted almost entirely of foreigners. Lefort, whose military experience was scanty but who was competent at everything, undertook to muster a regiment of twelve thousand men, and was completely successful. Five colonels were placed under his command, and he found himself all at once general of this little army, which had in fact been levied as much against the Streltsi as against the enemies of the state.

What is worthy of note here, and what thoroughly confutes the foolhardy error of those who maintain that the revocation of the Edict of Nantes had cost France but few men, is the fact that one third of this army-called-regiment consisted of French refugees. Lefort drilled his brand-new force as to the manner born.

Peter wanted to see one of those sham wars, one of those encampments which were just beginning to be introduced in peacetime. A fort was constructed; one detachment of his new troops was to defend it, the other to attack it. The difference between these maneuvers and all others was that instead of a mock battle they fought a real one, in which some soldiers were killed and many were wounded. Lefort, who was commanding the attackers, himself received a serious wound. These bloody games were intended to toughen the troops, but prolonged labors and even prolonged setbacks were required before success was achieved. The czar combined these martial entertainments with the care he was lavishing on his navy, and, just as he had made Lefort, who had never held a command, a general, so he made him an admiral without his ever sailing a ship. Peter, however, considered him worthy to do both. It is true that the admiral had no fleet and the general had no army other than his regiment.

Little by little, they reformed the greatest failing of the Russian military, namely, the independent spirit of the boyars who led their peasant militias. It was the authentic governance of the Franks, Huns, Goths, and Vandals, the peoples who vanquished the Roman Empire in its decadence, but who would have been annihilated had they come up against the old, disciplined Roman legions or armies like those of today.

Before long, Admiral Lefort no longer held a totally empty title. He had some Dutchmen and Venetians build galleys, and even two warships of approximately thirty guns apiece, at the mouth of the Voronezh, which flows into the Don. These vessels were capable of sailing downstream and holding the Crimean Tartars in check. Hostilities with these tribesmen were continually breaking out. In 1689, the czar had to make a decision: whether to wage war on Turkey, Sweden, or China. We must begin by showing on what terms he was with China, as well as describing the first peace treaty the Chinese ever made.

❖ The Funeral Oration of Archbishop Theophanes for Peter the Great (March 10, 1725)[1]

What is this? To what Times have we liv'd? O Countrymen! What do we fee? What are we doing? Do we interr PETER the Great? Or is this an Illufion? Or is it not a Vifion? Or are we not in a Dream? Oh too true is the Occafion of our sorrow! Oh too apparent is our Lofs! The Author of our innumerable Bleffings and Joys, having as it were raifed *Ruffia* from a State of Death; or rather as a Father, begot and nourifh'd and exalted it to the higheft Pitch of Power and Glory: This true Father of his Country, whom for his Merits the loyal Sons of *Ruffia* wifh'd to be exempt from Death, and with Regard to his Age and Conftitution, we hop'd would yet have liv'd many Years, contrary to our Wifhes and Hopes hath ceas'd to live. O the fevere Stroke to us! He then ceas'd to live, when after fo many Fatigues, fuch infinite Cares, Difquietudes and Dangers; after fo many and different

---

1. Reprinted from James Cracraft, ed. *For God and Peter the Great, The Works of Thomas Consett, 1723–1729* (New York, Columbia University Press, 1982, pp. 279–287.

Kinds of Deaths efcap'd, he began to live! We fee hence fufficiently how we have provoked thee, O our God! And how greatly we have abufed thy Forbearance! O unworthy and wretched that we are! O the Bulk of our Offences! He who fees not this is blind; but if he fees and regards not, has a Heart of Stone.

But why do we aggravate our Grief and Sorrow, which it becomes us rather to moderate? But how is this proffible to be done? To recollect and recount his great Talents, Exploits, and Actions, will but open our Wounds afrefh, and revive more fenfibly our Grief for the lofs of fo great a Bleffing. This is a Lofs indeed not to be forgot, unlefs we can be fuppos'd to fall into a Lethargy, or a dead Sleep.

Of whom, of what, and how great a Man are we depriv'd? Lo! this *O Ruffia,* was thy *Sampfon!* Such a Man as was never expected to be feen in thee, whom the whole World admir'd! He found thee Impotent and Feeble, and made thee according to the Import of his own Name, firm and durable as a Rock: he found a Soldiery Mutinous at Home, and Cowards in the Field, and the Scoff of Foes, and has now reform'd and made them a Defence to their Country, formidable to their Enemies, and to carry along with them every where Terrour and Triumph. Whilft he defended his own Country, he at the fame Time reftor'd it to its full Poffeffions, by the recovery of Territories it had formerly loft, and amplify'd and enlarg'd it, by the Acceffion and Conqueft of new Provinces: whilft he fubdu'd our Enemies that rofe up againft us, he at the fame Time vanquifh'd thofe that wifh'd us Evil; and having even ftop'd the Mouths of the Envious, he hath engag'd the whole World in his Praifes.

Behold, O *Ruffia,* thy firft *Japhet!* who has effected and brought to Perfection what was never before known with thee, Shipbuilding and Navigation; a Fleet new in the World, but not inferiour to the oldeft; fo much above Expectation, fo far furpaffing the Admiration of the whole World: hath open'd thee a Paffage to the Ends of the Earth, and extended thy Power and Glory to the Extremities of the Ocean, as far as thy Interefts can reach, or Juftice carry thee; and the Dominion of thy Scepter, which heretofore only totter'd on the Land, he has now fix'd fure and fteddy on the Seas.

Behold thy *Mofes,* O *Ruffia,* famous for fo many excellent Inftitutions! Are not his Laws the ftrong Bulwarks of Juftice, and indiffoluble Fetters of Iniquity? Are not his Statutes a plain and evident Light to thy Paths? Are not the High Senate, and the other inferiour Colleges and Courts of Judicature founded by him, as fo many Luminaries to direct thee in the Queft and Purfuit of thy Interefts and Advantages, in the Prevention and Removal of Evils, in preferving and maintaining Peace and Quiet to good Men, and in reftraining the Licentious? That it is indeed a kind of Doubt with us under what Confideration he is moft to be Prais'd; whether as he was belov'd, and merited the Efteem of honeft and good Men, or as he was dreaded and hated by diffolute Knaves and Villains.

Behold, O *Ruffia*, this thy *Solomon*, whom God endow'd w'th extraordinary Wifdom and Prudence! Proofs of this are as many as were the numerous Philofophical Experiments he himfelf made, and demonftrated by his own Obfervations, and which he communicated to his People; as alfo an amazing variety of Arts and Trades, the Rudiments of which we were before wholly unacquainted with. Add hereto the Ranks and Degees amongft us, the civil Ordinances, the decent Forms of Behaviour, the Rules of agreeable Modes and Fafhions, the Statelinefs and Beauty of our Houses, and the Decorum of living in them, wholly chang'd from what was formerly, which all concurr in the Evidence of his excellent Wifdom. And fuch is the delicate Form in which our Country now appears, with Regard to the Ornaments both of Body and Mind, that with juft Admiration we fee it alter'd incomparable for the better, and quite another Face of Things than was before.

Behold, O Church of *Ruffia*, both thy *David* and thy *Conftantine!* The Eftablifhment of a Synod to adminifter thy greateft and weighteft Affairs, is owing to him; the Inftructions of Preachers, and the writing of religious Books was the Effect of his Care. O what Concern did he exprefs, that the Way of Salvation was not better underftood! How great his Zeal againft fuperftition, delufive Factions, ftupid, mifchievous, and deftructive Schifms! How great his Defire and Endeavour to cultivate Learning in the Priefthood, the true Worfhip of God in the People, and to reform the Practice of all!

But O the Illuftrious Man, equal to the Characters of fo many great Names! How fhall we compafs in a fhort Speech his innumerable Praifes? Yet our very Sorrow and Grief will not permit us to enlarge upon the, extorting at prefent from us only Tears and Groans. In Time this fharp Thorn which pricks us to the Heart may poffibly be blunted, and then we may fpeak more amply of his Virtues and Exploits. Tho' all we can fay will never be enough, nor are we able to equal his Merits with our Commendations of them; yet by this fhort Defcription and touching, in a Manner, but the Hem of his Garment, we fee my moft Honourable Hearers! We miferab'e unfortunate Men fee what a Man hath left us, and what a Parent we are deprived of!

But, O *Ruffians*, Let us not quite fink under the Preffure of our Affliction! This great Monarch and Father hath not wholly forfaken us; he hath left us, but not Poor and Indigent, the immenfe Riches and Fruits of his Atchievments, and Glory are ftill with us; fuch as he has made his *Ruffia*, fuch it will continue: he hath made it amiable to its Friends; it will be belov'd by them: he hath made it terrible to its Enemies; it will remain fo: he hath made it glorious through the whole World; it will never ceafe to be glorious: he hath left us Directions and Regularions, Spiritual, Civil, and Military; therefore, though his Body is feperated from us, his Spirit remains with us.

Even in his laft Farewel he has not left us deftitute; Can we account ourfelves Orphans, when we look on his Auguft Succeffor, next to him, our chief Support in his Life-time, and after his Deceafe our Governour like and equal to him; on You, our moft Gracious and moft Potent Sovereign, the great Heroine and Monarch, and the Mother of all *Ruffia?* The whole World is agreed, that your being a Woman does not obftruct your Refemblance, in the Qualities of your Mind, to *PETER* the Great. For all confefs you to be endow'd by God with the true Qualifications of Government, Wifdom, and a moft tender Motherly Difpofition towards all. And after both thefe eminent Endowments, and many more excellent Talents were confirm'd and perfected in you, not only by your conjugal and conftant Cohabitation with fo great a Monarch, but even by your Admiffion into his moft intimate Councils, and by an infeperable Participation of his Fatigues and Dangers; wherein you were exercis'd for a Courfe of many Years, like Gold try'din the Fire: he adjudg'd it not Recompence enough that you was made the Partner of his Bed, unlefs he alfo provided and appointed that you fhould fucceed to his Crown, his Scepter and his Throne. How fhould we not hope then, that you will ratify what he has done, that you will perfect what he has left undone, and preferve the whole in a good Conftitution?

But O Madam! You that have the Soul and Spirit of a Man! Rouze up your wonted Courage, and do your utmoft to furmount this unfupportable Grief; notwithftanding it is doubl'd by the Deprivation of a beloved Daughter, and like a grievous Wound, beyond Meafure, fmarting with a frefh Stroke. And fuch as you have been obferv'd by all to be, when you accompany'd *PETER* in his Wars, his conftant Companion in his all Toils and Enterprizes, you fhould now endeavour to be in this moft fevere Difpenfation.

And you, the Honourable Affembly of every Rank and Vocation! Ye Sons of *Ruffia!* Continue to adminifter Confolation to your *Sovereign* and *Mother,* by your Loyalty and Obedience; and fupport yourfelves with an undoubted Affurance, that you fee the Spirit of *PETER* animating and informing the Perfon of our Monarch, that all of *PETER* is not fled from us.

In a Word, let us proftrate ourfelves before our God, who hath thus vifited us, that he our Merciful God, and the Father of all Confolation, would vouchfafe to difpenfe his Grace and Support to her Majefty, to her dear Offsping her Daughters, to her Grand-Children, Nieces, and the reft of her Auguft Houfe.

And may he wipe away this Flood of Tears, and fweeten this Bitternefs at the Heart, with the Refrefhments of his Grace; and Cheer all of us with his Mercy and Loving-kindnefs.

And Thou, O *Ruffia!* In confidering what a Prince thou haft loft, reflect how Great he has left thee.

Printed in St. Petersburgh, March the 14th, 1725.

Chapter Two

ANNA AND ELIZABETH

*Under the successors of Peter the Great, a
wide spectrum of Western influences began to
find fertile soil in Russia. Many of these influences were enriching, yet the indiscriminate
adoption of Western customs and attitudes simply because they were Western produced certain negative results. The emulation of Western art and ar-
chitecture, as well as the manufacture or importation of Western products
was extremely expensive. Increasingly, the serfs were forced to bear the burden of the lavish lifestyles adopted by the nobility in cities such as St. Petersburg and Moscow.*

*For approximately forty years following the death of Peter the Great, the
intrigues of foreign opportunists (especially North Germans) and the greedy
and volatile palace guard dominated the Russian court. Despite the law of
succession initiated by Peter, according to which the ruler could appoint his
heir (in imitation of the custom of the "Five Good Emperors" of ancient
Rome), which he hoped would provide a measure of stability to the court,
the throne in this period was held by several weak monarchs who were
dominated by powerful aristocrats. Among the principal power brokers of
this era were Prince Alexander Menshikov, who influenced Peter's successor
(and second wife), Catherine I (1725–27), and Count Biron, who dominated
during the brief reign of Ivan VI (1740–41). However, two monarchs stand
out in this period, both of whom were women: Anna (1730–40) and Elizabeth (1741–62).*

*Initially, Duchess Anna of Courland (niece of Peter the Great) was cho-
sen to ascend the throne by the Council of State, which was dominated by
the powerful Dolgorukii and Golitsin families, on condition that she accept a
number of qualifications of her authority. Our first passage in this section is
the list of qualifications to which Anna agreed before ascending the throne
(which qualifications she later abrogated), recorded by the German general
Manstein.*

*Empress Elizabeth, Peter the Great's daughter, came to the throne during
a surge of anti-foreign sentiment in 1741, in which many of the Westerners
who had come to St. Petersburg during the reign of Anna and before were
purged. Elizabeth subsequently appointed ethnic Russians to posts formerly
occupied by members of the Western emigré community. Like her father, she
sought to improve the Russian economy through direct government action.*

Thus, a tariff barrier was raised to protect Russian-made products within the domestic economy and government-sponsored banks were opened to finance industrial and commercial expansion. Following the example set by her father in the great Northern War, Elizabeth brought Russia actively into Western European political struggles, by siding with France and Austria against Prussia and Britain in the Seven Years' War (her nephew and successor, Peter III, however, idolized Frederick the Great of Prussia and actually switched Russia over to the side of Prussia and Britain—the eventual winners of the war). Our second passage in this section is a description of Elizabeth's accession, according to General Manstein.

✤ *Anna's Accession*[1]

The council of state, the senate, and such of the principal generals of the army as were then at Moscow, assembled immediately after the decease of Peter II., and sat in close committee in a chamber of the palace of the Kremlin. The High-chancellor Golofkin announced to the assembly the death of the emperor, and as soon as he had done speaking, the Prince Demetrius Michaelowitz Galitzin got up, and said, that "since, by the demise of Peter II., the whole male line of Peter I. was extinct, and Russia had suffered extremely by despotic power, propped up by the great number of foreigners that had been brought in by Peter I., it would be highly expedient to limit the supreme authority by salutary laws, and not confer the imperial crown on the new empress that should be chosen except under certain conditions;" concluding with putting the question to the whole assembly, whether "they did not approve this proposal?" They all assented to it, without any the least opposition. Upon which the Prince Basilius Loukitz Dolgorouki proposed the Duchess Dowager of Courland; alleging, that as the crown was now falling to a female, it was but just to prefer the daughter of the Czar Iwan, the elder brother of Peter I., to those of this emperor; that though the Duchess of Mecklenburg was the eldest, it was to be considered that she was married to a foreign prince, whereas the Duchess of Courland was actually a widow, and only thirty years of age; so that she might marry, and give heirs to Russia.

The true reason, however, for preferring the Duchess of Courland was, that she being at Mattau, the remoteness of that place would afford time for the firmer establishment of the proposed republican system.

All the votes then united in her favor, and it was agreed, that the council of state, which at that time consisted of seven members, of whom the majority were Dolgoroukis or their relations, should have the whole power; and the assembly framed the following articles:

1st. That the Empress Anne was to reign only in virtue of the resolves, after deliberation, of the supreme council.

2nd. That she should not declare war nor make peace on her own authority.

3d. That she should not lay on any new tax, or bestow any post or place of consequence.

---

1. Reprinted from Christof Von Manstein, *Contemporary Memoirs of Russia From the Year 1727 to 1744* (London, Frank Cass and Company, LTD, 1856), pp. 27–30, 38–39.

Photo: Fountain at the Summer Palace in St. Petersburg, which eventually empties into the Gulf of Finland.

4th. That she should punish no gentleman with death unless he was first duly convicted of his crime.

5th. That she should not confiscate any one's property.

6th. That she should not alienate or dispose of any lands belonging to the crown.

7th. That she should not marry, nor choose an heir, without asking, upon all these points, the consent of the supreme council.

The assembly then chose three members to notify to the empress her accession to the throne, and to propose to her the conditions under which she was to reign. On the part of the council was deputed the Prince Basilius Loukitz Dolgorouki; on the part of the senate, the Prince Michael Galitzin; and on the part of the nobility, the Lieutenant-general Leontew. In the instructions given to these deputies, it was enjoined upon them to require of the empress that she should sign the above articles, and that she should not bring her favourite, Biron, gentleman of the chamber, with her to Moscow.

The Count Osterman, who had not for one moment quitted the emperor during his illness, retired to his own house, overwhelmed with fatigue, and feigning sickness, that he might not be at the assembly of the council and senate, though he was vice-chancellor of the empire. It was by means of these sicknesses, which occurred at proper times, that this minister kept his ground so long in Russia.

Notwithstanding these precautions taken by the supreme council, the Princess Elizabeth might probably have been empress, if in the first moments she would but have followed the advice of her surgeon, since Count Lestock. As soon as he learnt the death of the emperor, he entered the chamber of the princess, who was asleep; and waking her, pressed her strongly to assemble the guards, show herself to the people, and, going at once to the senate, assert her title to the crown. But she could not be prevailed on to stir out of her room. Perhaps she had not, at that time, firmness enough to execute so great an enterprise. We have since seen her show more boldness and decision. But just then she preferred innocent amusements to the glory of reigning; and very certain it is that if she had not been molested in the reign of Anne, she would have continued to prefer the tranquillity of a private life to the burthen of a crown. It is also true, that at that time her party was far from strong; many of the grandees of the empire saying publicly, that she was too young to be empress. Indeed, after this princess had ascended the throne, she herself talking one day with General Keith, on his telling her that he much wondered her majesty had not asserted her right to the crown immediately on the death of Peter II., she replied, "I am very glad I did not: I was too young, and my people would never have borne with me."

The council imagined they had taken sufficient precaution against the restoration of despotic government, having exacted from the whole army an oath, that it would not serve the empress but at the discretion of the senate. Moreover, before the assembly broke up, they forbade on pain of death, the acquainting the new empress with any thing that had been debated or resolved. She was not to receive advice of her election, and of the conditions under which she was to mount the throne, but at first hand from the deputies. Notwithstanding these precautions, the Lieutenant-general Jagouzinski despatched his aide-de-camp, M. Samarokow, to Mittau that night to apprise the empress of every thing. He wrote to her, and entreated her to hasten her departure from Mittau as soon as the deputies should have had their audience; to submit to all the conditions that might be required of her; and for the rest, to trust to his counsels; that, in the meanwhile, until her arrival at Moscow, he would use his best endeavors to increase the party of such as were not at all pleased with this government by the council of state; that his father-in-law, the High-chancellor Golofkin, was already on her side; and that on the arrival of her majesty everything would turn out according to her wish.

In the speech which the empress made when she assumed absolute sovereignty, she had, it is true, promised to govern her states with mildness, and not to recur to rigorous punishments, unless in the last extremity. She could not, however, forget, that the Dolgoroukis had dared to aspire to place a princess of their own blood on the throne; and that, finding they could not bring that project to bear, they had employed all their arts to overturn the despotic power, and to remain in place, so as still to govern under another title.

All the princes Dolgorouki, who had been concerned in the schemes of the council of state, were arrested at one and the same time. They were tried and accused of various crimes; among others, of having diverted the emperor from the study of sciences worthy of him, and the acquisition of knowledge necessary for reigning; of having ruined his health by over-frequent hunting parties, and consequently caused his premature death. It was also added, that, in order to accomplish their ambitious ends, they had projected to marry the emperor to a princess of their family before he was of sufficient age; and that they had bestowed the greatest offices in the state on their relations and creatures, and so on. The empress, for this time, granted them their lives. The princess that had been betrothed to the emperor was shut up in a convent. The Prince Iwan, who had been high-chamberlain and favourite, was, together with his father, his uncle, and all their nearest relations, banished, some to their estates, others to Beresowa, or other remote places in Siberia; with a prohibition against any correspondence being held with them without the express leave of the court.

✤ *The Empress Elizabeth*[1]

The next morning, when Lestock waited as usual upon the princess, he presented a card to her; on one side of which there was drawn with a pencil, the princess Elizabeth with an imperial crown on her head; and on the reverse of it, the same princess, with a nun's veil, surrounded by racks and gibbets; with this he said to her: "Your highness must now absolutely choose one of these two things, to be empress, or to be put into a convent, and to see your faithful servants perish under tortures." He exhorted her then not to delay a moment; and, accordingly, the resolution was taken to proceed to extremities that very night. Lestock did not fail to acquaint with the fact all who were of their party. At midnight, the princess, accompanied by Woronzow and Lestock, repaired to the barracks of the grenadiers of the Preobraschenski regiment, thirty of whom were, as has been observed, personally in the plot. These assembled others to the number of 300, non-commissioned officers and privates. The princess, in a few words, declared her intention to them, and asked their assistance. They all, to a man, consented to devote themselves to her. Their first step was to seize the officer of the grenadiers, who lay in the barracks;—his name was Grews, and he was a Scotchman;—after which they took an oath of fidelity to the princess. She then put herself at their head, and marching straight to the winter-palace, entered, with part of those that followed her, into the guard-rooms, without meeting any the least resistance. There she told the officers the reason of her coming. They made no show of opposition, and left her to act as she pleased. Sentinels were then posted at all the doors and avenues. Lestock and Woronzow penetrated with a detachment of grenadiers into the apartments of the grand-duchess, and made prisoners of her and her husband, her children, and the favourite, that was lodged near them. As soon as this was done, several detachments were sent to seize marshal Munich, his son, who was lord steward of the household to the grand-duchess, count Osterman, count Golofkin, count Loewenwolde, baron Mengden, and some other persons of less consequences. All these prisoners were carried to the palace of the princess. She sent Lestock to marshal Lacy, to acquaint him with what she had done, and to tell him that he had nothing to fear; ordering him at the same time to come to her directly.

The senate, and all the grandees of the empire, were convened at the palace of the new empress; and, at break of day, all the troops were assembled before it, where, after the declaration to them, that the Princess Elizabeth had seated herself on the throne of her father, the oath of fidelity was ten-

1. Reprinted from Christof Von Manstein, *Contemporary Memoirs of Russia From the Year 1727 to 1744* (London, Frank Cass and Company, LTD, 1856), pp. 321–326.

dered to them, and taken without any difficulty being made, so that everything was presently in as great tranquillity as before.

The same day, the empress quitted the house in which she had resided till then, and took possession of the imperial palace.

After the revolution by which the duke of Courland fell, every one was delighted; not a sound but of joy was heard in the streets. Very different was it upon this occasion; upon every face might be seen consternation depicted; every one was in fear either for himself or some member of his family, and complete confidence was not restored till some days afterwards. It is certain that if in the course of the first forty-eight hours, a man of resolution had been found to put himself at the head of some troops, he might have dethroned the new empress.

There can hardly be any one who, in reading the account of this event, will fail to be astonished at the mistakes committed on both sides. Without the total blindness of the grand-duchess, the attempt must have miscarried. I have mentioned, that she had repeated information sent her even from foreign countries. Count Osterman one day had himself carried to her, and acquainted her with the secret conferences of La Chetardie and Lestock. Instead of an answer to the purpose of what he was telling her, she showed him a new frock she had just had made for the little emperor. The very same evening that she had the explanation above related with the Princess Elizabeth, the marquis de Botta spoke to her as follows: "Your imperial highness has neglected assisting the queen my mistress, notwithstanding the alliance between the two courts; but as there is now no remedy for that, I hope that, with the assistance of God, and of our other allies, we shall get out of our difficulties: but at least, madam, do not at this moment neglect taking care of yourself. You are on the brink of a precipice. In the name of God! save yourself! save the emperor! save your husband!"

All these exhortations did not produce any effect, nor did the grand-duchess make the least move to secure her throne. Her imprudence went still farther. Her husband told her, the night before the revolution, that he had certain information concerning the conduct of the Princess Elizabeth; that he was going to give orders to post picquets in the streets, and to have Lestock taken up; but the grand-duchess hindered him, by her answer, that she would vouch for the innocence of the princess. Her reasons were, that when she spoke to her of her conferences with La Chetardie, she had not in the least changed countenance, but had wept bitterly. She has had time to repent of her credulity.

The false steps on the side of the Princess Elizabeth were not less numerous. Lestock had talked in several places, and before different people of the great change that was soon to take place. The rest of her party were not more trustworthy; the most of them were but soldiers of the guard, and consequently of the lower classes,—men of little power of reticence in an affair of this importance. Even the princess herself did many things for which she would have been arrested under the reign of the Empress Anne. She often took a walk in the barracks of the guards; nay, she suffered some of the common soldiers to get behind her open sledge, and talk familiarly to her as she was drawn along in it through the streets of Petersburg. She had every day some grenadiers in her palace, and upon all occasions affected to make herself popular. But a fatal blindness prevailed with Anne and her party, Providence having decided that this attempt should succeed.

On the day of the revolution, the new empress declared by a manifesto, that she had ascended her father's throne, in virtue of her hereditary right, and, as the lawful sovereign, had caused the usurpers to be seized.

Three days afterwards, another manifesto was published, intended to prove her having an unquestionable title to the imperial crown. It was also specified therein, that as neither the Princess Anne nor her husband had any right to the throne of Russia, they should be sent back, with their family, to Germany. They were made to leave Petersburg with all their domestics, under an escort of guards commanded by general Soltikoff, who had been at the head of the police in the time of the Empress Anne; but they got no farther than Riga, where they were arrested and imprisoned in the citadel for a year and half. From thence they were transferred to the fort of Düna-munde; and at length, instead of being permitted to go to Germany, they were brought back into Russia, and imprisoned, first at Oranienburg, a town built by prince Menzikoff, afterwards at Kolmogori, a place situated in one of the islands of the Dwina, eighty versts from Archangel. This is the town in which the grand-duchess died in childbed, in the month of March, 1746. Her body was brought to Petersburg, and buried in the convent of St. Alexander Newsky.

Chapter Three

CATHERINE THE GREAT AND THE ENLIGHTENMENT

Elizabeth was succeeded by her politically-untalented nephew Peter III in 1762. Peter was despised by many courtiers, and early plans to assassinate him before he could inherit the throne were only stymied because the suddenness of Elizabeth's death caught the conspirators off guard. Even his German-born wife Catherine (formerly Sophia of Anhalt-Zerbst) wished to depose him and cooperated with the conspirators against him. Shortly after ascending the throne Peter was banished to the estate at Ropsha and murdered. Catherine was then placed on the throne by courtiers who believed that they could control her. Her indomitable will, however, was too great for those who sought to control the court through intrigue. An ambitious woman, Catherine employed her charm fully to attract supporters. She was reputed to have had a number of affairs, some of which were as much matters of political expediency as personal companionship.

Catherine was fascinated by the philosophical and political ideas of the French Enlightenment, and cultivated ties with Voltaire (with whom she corresponded) and Diderot (by whom she was visited in 1773–74). Catherine's jurists, influenced by Montesquieu, drafted The Instruction on the Codification of the Law (Nakaz). *She reorganized the provincial government in 1775, thus making local political, judicial, and financial bureaucracies more efficient. Catherine also expanded the Russian educational system and paid particular attention to women, appointing Princess Dashkova as head of the Academy of Sciences.*

Catherine directed an aggressive foreign policy against the Ottoman Turks, gaining control of the Black Sea coast as far as the Bug River and then as far as the Dnestr River in two wars (1768–74 and 1787–92). Catherine also conquered the Crimea and thrice participated in the partition of Poland (1772, 1793, 1795).

In 1772 the Cossack leader Emelian Pugachev rose up against Catherine, claiming to be Peter III and stirring up the peasants against the nobles. She had previously considered herself to be an "enlightened monarch," who ruled for the good of her subjects. Catherine was horrified, however, when the uprising by Pugachev and the peasants took on the aspect of a civil war against the nobility led by a pretender to the throne (reminiscent of the False Dmitri). The character of her reign changed considerably when the revolt was quelled in 1774. In order to gain the support of the nobles, she freed them from the Table of Ranks. Finally, many of the progressive attitudes which she held in the early part of her reign were further debilitated by the American Revolution and abandoned when she learned of the excesses of the French Revolution.

Our first passage in this section illustrates Catherine's view of her powers over the Russian people. The text is her official title as presented in the Charter of the Rights, Freedoms and Privileges of the Noble Russian Dvorianstvo *(April 21, 1775), translated by Paul Dukes. The next three passages were written by Catherine herself in her memoirs (translated by Katharine Anthony); the first of these reflects the interests and concerns of the future monarch on her wedding day, and shows us something of Catherine the woman; the second concerns her desire to create coherent territorial divisions, or* gubernias *within her empire; and the third shows us how she wished to be remembered to posterity, in the epitaph which she composed for herself.*

The fifth passage is an excerpt from the Manifesto on the Freedom of the Nobility, *issued February 18, 1762 (translated by Dukes). Our sixth passage is an excerpt from the previously-mentioned* Charter of Rights *concerning the honors and rewards due to the nobility (translated by Dukes). During the early phase of her reign when she was interested in the political philosophy of the Enlightenment, S. E. Desnitskii drafted a proposal for Catherine regarding the division of political power within government, and we have extracted a passage from this document as our seventh passage (translated by Dukes). The eighth and ninth passages consist of several edicts issued by Pugachev in the name of Peter III during the uprising of 1772–74, as well as the interrogation of Pugachev (translated by Dukes). Our tenth and eleventh passages are taken from* The Institution of the Administration of the Provinces of the Empire *(1775) and the* Nakaz, *respectively (translated by Dukes). Catherine's greatest general was Alexander R. Suvorov, whose brilliant strategies won glorious victories for Russia on many foreign battlefields. Our twelfth passage is taken from Suvorov's* Art of Victory, *translated by Phillip Longworth.*

Alexander Radishchev has been termed "the first Russian radical" because of the social consciousness and concern which he exhibited towards the serfs during Catherine's reign, particularly in the context of the Pugachev uprising. The thirteenth passage is taken from Radishchev's A Journey from St. Petersburg to Moscow *(translated by Leo Wiener).*

✤ *Catherine's Official Title*[1]

Through God's beneficent kindness, We Catherine the Second, Empress and Autocrat of All the Russias, of Moscow, of Kiev, of Vladimir, or Novgorod, Chernigov, Riazan, Polotsk, Rostov, Iaroslavl, Berlozersk, Tsarina of Kherson-Tavricheskii, Sovereign of Pskov and Grand Duchess of Smolensk, Princess of Estonia, Livonia, Karelia, Tver, Iugorsk, Perm, Viatka, Bolgariia and others; Sovereign and Grand Duchess of Nizhnii Novgorod, Chernigov, Riazan, Polotsk, Rostov, Iaroslavl, Verlozersk, Udoriia, Obdoriia, Kondiia, Vitebsk, Mstislavl and of all the Northern Territories Lady and Sovereign of the Land of Iveriia, the Kargalian and Georgian Tsars and Land of Kabarda, of the Cherkassian and Mountain princes and others the hereditary Sovereign and Proprietrix.

It is known to all the people that in this title of Our Autocracy are not included the kingdoms, principalities, provinces, towns or the lands of others not subject to us or putative; but rather Our largest possessions with their shortest titles are indicated, because they are many.

---

1. Reprinted by permission of the publishers from Paul Dukes, trans., *Russia Under Catherine the Great, Volume One: Select Documents on Government and Society* (Newtonville, Mass., Oriental Research Partners, 1978), p. 162.

✤ *Catherine on Her Wedding Day*[1]

The nearer my wedding day approached, the sadder I became, and often I felt obliged to weep without exactly knowing why. Although I concealed my tears as well as I could, my women who were always near naturally could not fail to notice them and took pains to cheer me up.

On the day before the 21st of August, we moved from the Summer Palace to the Winter Palace. Up to that time I had occupied, in the garden of the Summer Palace, the stone building on the Fontanka behind the pavilion of Peter the Great.

---

1. From *Catherine the Great* by Katharine Anthony. Copyright 1925 by Alfred A. Knopf, Inc. and renewed 1953 by Katharine Anthony. Reprinted by permission of the publisher, pp. 68–70.

Photo: Panoramic view of Vasilievskii Island across the Neva River, St. Petersburg.

My mother came to my room in the evening where we held a long and very friendly conversation. She preached to me a great deal about my future duties; we wept together a little and then parted very tenderly.

On the festive day I arose at six o'clock in the morning; at eight o'clock the Empress had me come to her apartments where I was to be dressed. I found a costume laid out in her state bedchamber and her palace ladies were already assembled. They began to dress my hair; my servant Timofei Yevreinov was curling my front hair with irons when the Empress entered. I rose to kiss her hand. Scarcely had she kissed me when she began to scold my attendant and forbade him to dress my hair with a frizzled bang. She wished to have my hair quite smooth because she believed the jewels would not stay on my head with this style of head-dress. Then she went out. But my servant was obstinate and would not give up his curling irons. He persuaded Countess Rumyantsov, who liked the frizzled hair and could not endure to have it so smooth, to present the case in favor of my toupet to the Empress. The Countess went back and forth two or three times between the Empress and the attendant, while I waited peacefully for what was to happen; finally the Empress, somewhat provoked, sent word that he should do what seemed best to him.

When my hair was dressed, the Empress put the grand ducal crown upon my head and then allowed me to put on as many of her jewels and my own as I wished. She withdrew and the ladies of the palace completed my costume in the presence of my mother. My dress was of silver glacé with silver embroidery at all the seams and astonishingly heavy.

About mid-day the Grand Duke entered the adjoining room. Towards three o'clock the Empress accompanied the Grand Duke and myself in her state coach to the Church of the Holy Virgin of Kazan where the Bishop of Novgorod performed the marriage ceremony. The Prince Bishop of Lueback held the wedding crown over the head of the Grand Duke and the Grand Master of the Hunt Count Alexei Razumovsky held it over mine. At my coronation later he also carried the crown.

We then returned to the Winter Palace where towards six o'clock we sat down to a banquet in the gallery. For this purpose a canopy had been raised. Under this sat the Empress with the Grand Duke on her right and with me on her left. One step lower and next to the Grand Duke sat my mother and next to me opposite to my mother was the place of my uncle, the Prince Bishop of Luebeck who was then in Petersburg.

After we had risen from the table the Empress retired to her apartment in order to give time for clearing away the table and arranging the gallery for the ball. When I rose from the table I feared a headache in consequence of the weight of the crown and the jewels, and I begged Countess Rumyantsov to remove the crown for a moment. I did not think that that would make any difficulties. But the Countess said she did not dare do that; she feared some evil omen might be attached to it. But when she saw that I was suffering she let herself be persuaded to speak with the Empress about it, who after some hesitation gave her consent. At last the crown was taken off until all was ready for the ball; then it was put on again. At this ball only polonaises were danced and it lasted altogether not more than an hour.

✤ The Gubernias[1]

The whole Empire was divided into the following gubernias: Moscow, Nizhni-Novgorod, Kazan, Astrachan, Siberia, Belgorod, Novgorod, Archangel St. Petersburg, Livonia, Viborg, and Kiev. Little Russia, that is, Tchernigov and Novgorod Seversky, was managed by the Hetman. Each gubernia was divided into provinces, and each province had its district cities, in which the Vojevods and their chancellories were located. They received no salary but were permitted to draw their incomes from their occupations, although bribes were strictly forbidden.

The Senate appointed the Vojevods but did not know the number of cities in the Empire. When I asked for a list of the cities, they confessed their ignorance. Likewise the Senate had never since its installation owned a map of the whole Empire. When I was in the Senate I sent five rubles to the Academy of Sciences on the other side of the river and bought the atlas published by Cyrillov which I at once presented to the directing Senate.

From *Catherine the Great* by Katherine Anthony. Copyright 1925 by Alfred A. Knopt, Inc. and renewed 1953 by Katherine Anthony. Reprinted by permission of the publisher, p. 300.

✤ Catherine's Epitaph, Composed by Herself[1]

(1788)

Here lies
Catherine the Second
born in Stettin April 21/May 2, 1729.

In the year 1744 she went to Russia to marry Peter III.
At the age of fourteen she made the threefold resolution, to please her Consrot, Elisabeth, and the Nation.

---

1. From *Catherine the Great* by Katharine Anthony. Copyright 1925 by Alfred A. Knopf, Inc. and renewed 1953 by Katharine Anthony. Reprinted by permission of the publisher, p. 326.

She neglected nothing in order to succeed in this.

Eighteen years of tediousness and solitude caused her to read many books.

When she had ascended the throne of Russia, she wished to do good and tried to bring happiness, freedom, and prosperity to her subjects.

She forgave easily and hated no one.

She was good-natured and easy-going; she had a cheerful temperament, republican sentiments, and a kind heart.

She had friends.

Work was easy for her; she loved sociability and the arts.

✢ *The Manifesto on the Freedom of the Nobility*[1]

By the authority vested in Us by the Most High, by Our Highest Imperial Grace, We now and henceforth for all time and for all generations to come bestow on the whole Russian noble dvorianstvo freedom and liberty, and they may continue service both in Our Empire and in other European states allied to Us.

---

1. Reprinted by permission of the publishers from Paul Dukes, trans., *Russia Under Catherine the Great, Volume One: Select Documents on Government and Society* (Newtonville, Mass., Oriental Research Partners, 1978), p. 33.

✢ *The Charter of the Rights, Freedoms, and Privileges of the Noble Russian Dvorianstvo*[1]

The property received as a reward for its services has naturally made obligatory recourse to those generations of our dvorianstvo which could render their services from the foundations of Russia to our own days, as have the magnificent number of its worthy ancestors, intelligent men, skillful, brave and tireless, who

---

1. Reprinted by permission of the publishers from Paul Dukes, trans., *Russia Under Catherine the Great, Volume One: Select Documents on Government and Society* (Newtonville, Mass., Oriental Research Partners, 1978), pp. 163–164.

have fought with unshakable zeal and in many different ways against internal and external enemies of the faith, the monarch and the fatherland. But is the proof of the age of the services of their families and of the rewards for them to be found only in the property obtained? Honorary charters were granted before, after and at the same time as immovable property. They are the most concrete remains of their outstanding exploits, for which praise was given as Our most valuable gift and honour to such loving souls. Really where were honour-loving souls to be found more numerously than among the Russian nobility? And did not shame too confirm their obligations? Because shame and abuse are considered the most burdensome punishment to the noble and honour-loving souls, just as praise and distinction are considered the best reward. Such a way of thinking and the reasoning connected with it demand an increase of commensurate size in services, and with the flow of time and many changes in customs, distinctions and decorations in abundance. Coats-of-arms, diplomas for achievements and patents with ranks, together with decorations, have thus ensued as honorary charters granted as a commemoration for each family. In honour of virtues and services, knightly orders of All the Russias have been instituted, as the inscriptions generally attest. The Order of the Apostle Andrew the First-Called for faith and loyalty. Of the Saintly Martyr Catherine for love of the fatherland. Of the Saintly Lord Prince Alexander Nevskii for labour on behalf of the fatherland. And already in our days the service and bravery of the leading Russian warriors have encouraged us to decorate the victors with the Order established for them of the Great Victory-Bearer George and also to institute the Order of the Holy Apostle Prince Vladimir as a reward for military and civil services which contribute to the general benefit, honour and glory.

✥ S. E. Desnitskii's Proposal on the Division of Powers[1]

To make the laws, judge according to the laws and to put the judgement into execution—these three functions constitute the three powers, that is the legislative, judicial and executive power, on which powers depend almost all the administrative arrangements and all the main part of government in the state.

Consequently, the institution of these powers according to the time and place must constitute for those subjects summoned to such business the first object of their discussion, particularly during the presently intended revival in Russia.

---

1. Reprinted by permission of the publishers from Paul Dukes, trans., *Russia Under Catherine the Great, Volume One: Select Documents on Government and Society* (Newtonville, Mass., Oriental Research Partners, 1978), p. 48.

Care must be taken with the institution of these powers, that one power does not overstep its limit into another and also that each of these powers should have its supervisors, so that it will always be subject to their concern.

If these powers are first of all happily arranged and delimited by statute, all other regulations which seem necessary may be made in completion of this main business.

In what manner such an establishment may be put into effect, I dare to most humbly submit my plan to your imperial highness.

✣ *Edicts of Pugachev*[1]

1 December 1, 1773

Of his imperial highness the autocrat of all the Russians Peter Fedorovich, etc., etc., etc.

I want to keep in my God-given favour each man of those who now want to be subject and obedient to me by their own choice, all my true slaves. And if somebody in his misunderstanding remains aloof from my bounty given to all the people, then he will in the end receive from me great torment and will not be able at all to defend himself. Moreover, just as those who formerly gave their unswerving services to my grandfather the Emperor Peter the First, received no small rewards and praises for being in unfailing service till death for His Imperial Highness, so now I want with all my heart to hear about those who will give me their unswerving services, and after they have served, I will leave nobody without reward for their services. And whosoever recognises this my proven generosity, I have already endowed you all with this reward: land, fishing rights, woods, hives, beaver hunting rights and other advantages, also freedom. Moreover, I promise with the authority given to me as if from God, that you will henceforth suffer no oppressions.

And whosoever does not give any regard to my bounteous charity, such as: landlords, these breakers of the law and general peace, evildoers and opponents of my imperial will, deprive of all life, that is punish them with death, and take their homes and estates as a reward. And since the possessions and riches of those landlords, also their food and drink, have been at the expense of the peasants, thus they have had enjoyment, and your hardship and ruin. And now restored from the lost I have declared for you all, and I have gone over the whole

---

1. Reprinted by permission of the publishers from Paul Dukes, trans., *Russia Under Catherine the Great, Volume One: Select Documents on Government and Society* (Newtonville, Mass., Oriental Research Partners, 1978), pp. 122–123.

land on my own feet and have been created to give you mercy from the Creator. So, whosoever can now understand and reason out my charity given to you, and every one as my true slave, wants to see me. However, there are still not so many well-wishers for me, as disturbers of the general peace and haters. Now that the Almighty Lord with his inutterably just fate will again raise us to the all-Russian throne, so not one evil occasioned me will remain without retribution: and then everyone will recognise the weight of his crime. And although he will want to resort to lawful obedience and will attempt to promote and produce his unswerving services, nothing will be accepted: then he will sigh from the bottom of his heart and remember his eternal life, but then there will be no return. And whosoever receives this my gracious decree in his hands, he should immediately send it from town to town, from settlement to settlement, and explain the mercy afforded by me to all mankind and remember the eternal life, so that now and henceforth the thing explained above will be useful to all men.

Hereunder is signed thus with His Imperial Highness' own hand:

The Emperor and autocrat of all Russians,
Peter the Third.

Edict of Pugachev to the Peasants, 31 July 1774

By the grace of God, we Peter the Third, emperor and autocrat of all the Russians: etc., etc., etc.

It is announced for the information of all the people.

With this personal decree we bestow with our monarchical and paternal generosity all those formerly in the peasantry and subject to the landlords, be true slaves to our crown, and we reward you with the old cross and prayer, heads and beards, freedom and liberty, and you may be Cossacks for ever, without demands for recruit levies, poll and other money dues, possession of lands, woods and meadows and fishing rights, and salt lakes without tax and payment and we free all from the evils caused by nobles and bribe-taking town judges of the peasants, and taxes and burdens placed on all the people. And we wish all the salvation of their souls and quiet life in the world, for which we have tasted and suffered from the afore-mentioned villainous nobles exile and considerable poverty. And since now with the authority of God's Right Hand our name flourishes in Russia, therefore we order by this our personal decree: those who were formerly nobles in their estates, these opponents of our authority and disturbers of the empire and destroyers of the peasants catch, execute and hang and treat in the same way as they, not having Christianity, have dealt with you, the peasants. With the eradication of these opponents and villainous nobles, each may feel peace and a quiet life, which will continue for ever.

Given July 31 1774
Peter.

⚜ Testimony from Pugachev's Interrogation at Iaik Town (September 16, 1774)[1]

And so I set off towards Kazan, collecting more people from all places.

And before I arrived at Kazan, a detachment met me, which I smashed, and took all the people to myself. And the next day—another small number, which I also smashed without difficulty, and took the people, cannons and all the provisions to myself.

And coming up to Kazan, another detachment was seen on guard with one cannon. I destroyed it and took the bronze cannon, and gathered together some people, others ran away,

Coming up to Kazan, I stayed in camp, and wrote a decree to the Kazan governor that he should give himself up without a fight. And as there was no answer, I ordered forty loads of hay to be brought and make an attack. And although there was much opposition from many sides, I took Kazan. Going into it, I took all that was useful, and quite a few people were killed here. I freed the prisoners from the jail, where I found my wife Sof'ia, whom seeing, I said: "Hallo! [This is the] wife of my friend Pugachev who I lived with in poverty and he suffered for me" saying besides: "I shall not leave you, poor thing." And so I ordered her with the children to be taken with me, and I took them with me in a carriage to the last battle, which was near Chernyi Iar.

There were with me about ten more women, however they were not wives, but only dressed me and prepared food for me, and did all kinds of service.

Here several people of rank were flogged to death with whips. And this interrogation was carried out by Ovchinnikov and Davilin; Perfil'ev was at this time with the cannon. Later the Bashkirs burnt Kazan, and I left Kazan for camp. And as there was no forage here, I went to another place, where I heard that Mikhel'son was coming. And so I armed myself against him. And as my people were not in good order, I was forced to go back to my camp having lost six cannons and several people running away. And I stayed here forty-eight hours.

Later having put my people in good order, I went up to Mikhel'son near Kazan itself, to Arskoe Pole. And there was a battle with him. However Mikhel'son won and took all my artillery and all the baggage seized in Kazan and in other places.

---

1. Reprinted by permission of the publishers from Paul Dukes, trans., *Russia Under Catherine the Great. Volume One: Select Documents on Government and Society* (Newtonville, Mass., Oriental Research Partners, 1978), pp. 128–131.

And so I ran from the battle till night. And at night the Bashkirs—however many of them there were—all went from me to the Urals; there remained only the elder Kindzha.

The next day I ran away to the Volga, which we crossed. At this time I had five hundred people.

Having crossed the Volga, I set fire to a village because they gave no assistance, and I went along the Volga to the River Sura.

And before I reached it, there is a certain town, to which I sent the Cossack Chumakov to get horses, he took four officers there and without my authority hanged them. About them the inhabitants of that town coming up to me, said: "They did not resist, so why did they hang our lords?" To this I said: "Although the order was not given, there's no turning back now, let it be."

I came to Sura and stopped. The next day we went along the river, and went up to Saratov. And along the road in towns and settlements everywhere they met me with honour and some we executed through suspicion.

Coming to Saratov, I was joined by sixty Don men, and sixty Volga Cossacks; the commander of the Don men was a bear-mouth cornet and of the Volga men an oak cornet. Coming up to Saratov, I did not send a decree there, because they fired from cannons. And I supplied the hetmen Ovchinnikov with a detachment and took Saratov against opposition. Going in, taking cannons and howitzer, I went to camp and, staying twenty-four hours, went off to Kamyshin.

And before I got there several Tsaritsyn Cossacks came up to me. In Kamyshin there was no great opposition. The commander hid in the kremlin, but was taken by Ovchinnikov, and he and others were killed.

From there I went to the Antipovskaia settlement. And the Cossacks from that village went with me enthusiastically, also the Karavaiskie, and others, I do not remember from where.

And before I reached Dubovka a light detachment with Don Cossacks and Kalmyks met me. I smashed it. The officers of the light detachment about whom Ovchinnikov reported were overtaken and given a thrashing. And here ten cannons were taken, and I took as many people as there were, and went to Dubovka where I spent the night.

From there I went off towards Tsaritsyn. Before we reached it, three thousand Kalmyks came over into my subjects. Later Don Cossacks met with me and gave battle, and the Don Colonel was beaten.

When I came to Tsaritsyn itself, the Don Cossacks did not dare to give battle, although they were at the town. Later firing began from Tsaritsyn, and it was answered by me. But I turned round to the right side of Tsaritsyn to the place where the Cossacks stood and won them all over to me. The colonels of those Cossacks all went over to the town. There were six regiments of them.

And so I went past Tsaritsyn.

And at the first night camp the Don Cossacks went away man by man; I had not ordered them to be properly watched.

Coming away sixty versts from Tsaritsyn, a certain commander with a great force fell on me from behind, I do not know how. And at dawn there was a battle, at which I was beaten, lost almost all my people, cannons, two young daughters and all the baggage seized by me in many places.

I ran away with the Iaik Cossacks and some peasants, my wife and eldest son to the Volga. Hurriedly, I crossed to an island with my wife in a boat. And as it was necessary to cross further, Perfil'ev remained, I do not know why, and with him several people of my host.

Crossing from the Volga island to the flood-plain side and going off several versts, we stopped for the night.

From there I sent a colonel of my troop, Pustobaev, with one Cossack to seek the clothing lost by him, which he wanted to find, and Perfil'ev, but having set off he did not return.

I went off to the steppe with the Cossacks, of whom there were sixty-four people. Later we discussed: where shall we go? And after many discussions we agreed to go to the Uzen, and there, collecting more people, to go to the lower reaches of the Iaik, collect Cossacks there, take Gur'ev, board boats on the sea and sail to whatever hordes there were, to come to an agreement with them and return to Russia.

When we arrived at the Uzen, then the high-ranking people of my troop, agreeing with others arrested me. And as this was done beyond the River Uzen and carried out by not many people, because the larger part of my troop, the Cossacks, remained on the other side of the river, so I hoped to gallop off to them on a horse, and persuade them to stand up for me and tie up those who had arrested me. However when I galloped off, Ivan Tvorogov with others overtook me and caught me and led me a whole day and night on a bad horse.

And as they started to eat at a certain time, I seized a sabre and wanted to cut down those people who had arrested me first, that is, the instigators Fedulev and Chumakov. However I was overpowered and an even closer watch was kept on me.

And so they took me to Iaik Town.

Later there came to our troop a Cossack Lieutenant sent from the town to whom, talking with my former adherents, I said finally: "Why if you have thought of taking me into the town have you not bound me?" And so my adherents thought still at that time that I was sovereign and they did not want to bind me. Later the aforesaid Lieutenant put me in chains.

And so I was brought into Iaik Town to the secret commission, where I was interrogated about everything written above.

In conclusion I say this.

When I was still going to Kazan the Iaik Cossacks asked me to go to Moscow and further to which I agreed. When I was defeated near Kazan and crossed the Volga with a small number of people, although I collected a great troop, I had already decided not to go to Moscow, and to pick my way down, whithersoever it was agreed. Before we reached Saratov, the Cossacks talked me round to going with my whole troop, when it was large enough, to Iaik Town to spend the winter there and go again to Rus to complete my intention. The nobles and officers I killed mostly at the persuasion of the Iaik Cossacks, and I was myself by no means so cruel, but did not spare those who oppressed their peasants or the commanders—their subordinates; also I executed them without investigation, if any peasant reported landlords for tax exactions. I did not have soldiers for this in my troop because they were not suitable for my service. And when there was a necessity for infantry then I ordered the Cossacks to dismount to do everything like soldiers.

A further intention, to possess the whole Russian kingdom, I did not have because, considering myself, I did not think I was capable of government, because of my illiteracy. And I went because if I succeeded in somehow advancing myself or was killed in war,—surely I deserved death, it was better to die in war.

Savra Mavrin carried on the interrogation in Iaik Town in a special secret commission.

✢ *The Institution of the Administration of the Provinces of the Empire*[1]

Chapter I. Recommended establishment of the province. (articles 1–46)
For maximum efficiency, a province should have from 300 to 400 thousand souls. In the absence of Her Royal Highness, there is a controller or governor with two advisors. There is a criminal and civil court in each province, each with a president, two advisers and two assessors. Each province has a surveyor, an office of affairs of household management and another of management of state income. In the treasury office, there is the deputy of the controller or deputy governor, the director of the economy or of the management of the household, an adviser, two assessors and one provincial treasurer. In each province there is a higher land court, more than one if the size of the province demands it; it has a first and second president, and ten members. If necessary, the province is divided into counties; the provinces and counties are divided into districts. Each of the districts should have from 20 to 30 thousand souls and its own court, with a district judge, members of his

---

1. Reprinted by permission of the publishers from Paul Dukes, trans., *Russia Under Catherine the Great. Volume One: Select Documents on Government and Society* (Newtonville, Mass., Oriental Research Partners, 1978), pp. 143–145.

court, and two other members, and with a noble court of wards, presided over by the marshal of the nobility with the judge and members of the court. In each district, there is a lower land court with a land executive or captain, and two or three members, depending on the size of the district. In each district, there is one treasurer, one attested surveyor, one doctor, one apothecary, two assistant apothecaries and two apprentice apothecaries. In each town, where there is no commander, there is a chief of police, and in the capital, a head of police. In towns and suburbs, elders and judges of the courts of petty session stay on the former basis. Councils are in the suburbs only. In the towns, there will still be magistracies, each with a burgomaster and four councillors, and a court of wards presided over by the town head with two members of the town magistracy and the town elder. In the province, there will be one provincial magistracy, or more if the size of the province demands it, with a first and second president and six members. Depending on the circumstances, the governor may institute for smallholders and others from 10 to 30 thousand souls in number a court called the lower peasant justice, with one judge and eight members, of whom two are to sit in the lower land court and two in the court of equity for cases concerning their own areas. There are also one or two courts of higher peasant justice where circumstances demand, with a first and second president and ten members. There is also in each province a board of social welfare, with the governor himself as president and two members from the higher land court, two from the town magistracy and two from the higher peasant justice where it exists. In each province there is a court of equity with one judge, two dvoriane for cases concerning the nobility, two citizens for cases concerning townspeople, and two rural inhabitants for higher and lower peasant justice cases. In the provincial government and courts, there is a procurator, an attorney for state cases and an attorney for criminal cases, all of whom are to be found in the higher land court, the town magistracy and the higher peasant justice. In each district there is one attorney.

Chapter II *On ranks* (articles 47–58)
Ranks to be distributed to those actually serving as follows (if they have not already been awarded higher ranks): governor—fourth class; deputy governor, head of police, presidents of the criminal and civil courts—fifth class; the councillors of the provincial government, of the criminal and civil courts, the director of the management of the household, the councillor of the treasury office, the provincial procurator, the first and second presidents of the higher land court, and the judge of the court of equity—sixth class; the marshal of the nobility, the members and procurator of the higher land court, the provincial attorneys of state and criminal affairs, the first and second presidents of the provincial magistracy and of the higher peasant justice, the noble members of the court of equity—seventh class; the assessors of the offices, the provincial treasurer, the attorneys of state and criminal affairs in the higher land court, the procurators of the provincial magistracy and of the

higher peasant justice, the district judge, the chief of police and the provincial surveyor—eighth class; the land executive or captain, the judge of the peasant justice, members of the district court and district treasurer—ninth class; the noble members of the lower land court, the town head, the members of the provincial magistracy, the town members of the court of equity, the state and criminal attorneys of the provincial magistracy and of the higher peasant justice—tenth class; the first and second burgomasters of the town magistracy of the provincial capital and the district attorney—eleventh class; the first and second burgomasters and councillors of the provincial town magistracy—twelfth class; the burgomasters and councillors of the town magistracy in the suburbs—thirteenth class; the elders of the town, the judges of the court of petty sessions and councillors in the suburbs—fourteenth class; the presidents of the higher and lower peasant justice, the rural members of the lower land court and the court of equity—not to have rank, but not to be punished without trial, and to be considered first among their peers in their villages after service.

✤ *The Nakaz*[1]

Chapter 1st

6. Russia is a European Power.
7. Of which this is a Demonstration, The Changes undertaken in Russia by Peter the Great, met with the better Success, because the manners then existing (which had been brought in to use by the Conquest of foreign Powers, and the Mixture of various People) disagreed entirely with the nature of the Climate: So that Peter on introducing European Manners and Customs among a European People, found such Facility as he himself never expected.

Chapter 2nd

8. The Empire of Russia contains 32 degrees of Latitude, and 165 of Longitude on the Terrestrial Globe.

---

1. Reprinted by permission of the publishers from Paul Dukes, trans., *Russia Under Catherine the Great. Volume Two: Catherine the Great's Instruction (Nakaz) to the Legislative Commission, 1767* (Newtonville, Mass., Oriental Research Partners, 1977), pp. 43–44, 77, 118.

9. The Sovereign is absolute, for no other than absolute Powers vested in one Person, can be suitable to the Extent of so vast an Empire.

10. An extensive Empire demands absolute Power in the Person who rules it: it is necessary that Dispatch in the Decision of Affairs sent from distant places compensate for the Delay occasioned by their remoteness.

11. Any other than absolute Government, would not only be detrimental, but in the End destructive to Russia.

12. Another Reason is, that it is better to obey the Laws under the direction of one Master, than to be subject to the Wills of many.

13. What is the Object of absolute Government? Certainly not to deprive the People of their natural Liberty but to direct their Conduct in such manner that the greatest good may be derived from all their Operations.

14. That form of Government therefore which promotes this End more than any other, and infringes natural Liberty less than any other, is most conformable to the native Sentiments of reasonable Creatures, and at the same time corresponds best with the End constantly in View in the Establishment of Civil Societies.

15. The Intention and End of Absolute Government is the Glory of the Citizens, of the State, and of the Sovereign.

16. This Glory in a People under monarchical Government creates a sense of Liberty, which in such States, is capable of producing as many great Actions, and of contributing as much to the happiness of the Subjects, as Liberty itself.

❖

Chapter 12th

264. Of Population.

265. Russia not only has not Inhabitants enough but it contains immense Tracts of Land, neither peopled nor cultivated. And therefore it is impossible to devise sufficient means of Encouragement for increasing the Number of People in the State.

266. The Peasants have generally from 12 to 15 or 20 Children by one Marriage, but rarely does a fourth part of them attain to the Age of Maturity. Wherefore there must certainly be some Evil, either in their Diet or in their manner of Life, or in their Education, which is so destructive to this Hope of the State. How flourishing would the Situation of this Empire be, if it were possible by wise Institutions to avert or prevent this fatal Ruin.

❖

Chapter 22nd

628. The revenues which belong to the Sovereign are likewise of two kinds: they are his either as particular private landlord, or as head of state.
629. The Sovereign possesses the first in his own right.
630. But as Autocrat, he counts: (1) all the revenues of state property in its entirety; (2) impositions on the property of others.
631. A wise Autocrat never increases this last revenue without the greatest regret, and if he does so he watches carefully to see that the arrangement of the impositions is effected in proportion to the resources of the subjects, so that it does not exceed the measure of their ability from the point of view of possessions, and so that it does not burden the citizens more than they can naturally support or can be in justice demanded from them.

✥ *Suvorov's Art of Victory*[1]

'In an open battle there are three attacks. Firstly, in the weaker flank. It's unwise to tackle a strong flank covered by a wood. A soldier can pick his way across a marsh but it's harder to cross a river—you can't run across without a bridge. Secondly, an attack in the centre. This is useless unless the cavalry have room to use their sabres—otherwise they themselves are crushed together. Lastly, an attack in the rear, which is very good, but only for a small corps. It's difficult for any army to wheel round behind the enemy without his noticing. . . .

'In a field battle, fight in line against regulars and in squares against the Turks—no columns. But even against the Turks it could happen that a square of 500 men will have to tear through a mass of five or seven thousand with the help of flanking squares. In this case it should form into column—but up till now there has been no need for this. Then there are the godless, flighty, madcap French. They wage war on the Germans and others in columns. If we should happen against them we shall have to hit them with columns as well.'

---

1. Reprinted from Philip Longworth, *The Art of Victory. The LIfe and Achievements of Field Marshal Suvorov, 1729–1800* (New York, Holt, Rinehart, and Winston, 1966), pp. 217–218.

✛ *Radishchev on the Peasants*[1]

But who among us wears the fetters, who feels the burden of slavery? The agriculturists! The man who feeds us in our leanness and satisfies our hunger, who gives us health and prolongs our life, without having the right to dispose of what he cultivates nor of what he produces. But who has a greater right to a field than the man who cultivates it? Let us imagine that men have come into a wilderness to establish a community. Mindful of their need of sustenance, they divide up the uncultivated land. Who deserves a share in this division? Is it not he who knows how to plough the land, he who has the strength and determination requisite for the task? Can a country in which two thirds of the citizens are deprived of their civil rights and to some extent are dead to the law to be called happy? Can the civic condition of the peasant in Russia be called happy? Only an insatiable bloodsucker will say that the peasant is happy, for he has no conception of a better state of affairs.

---

1. Reprinted from Leo Wiener, trans. *A Journey from St. Petersburg to Moscow*, edited by Roderick Page Thayer (Cambridge, Mass., 1958), pp. 146–147.

Chapter Four

PAUL

Following Catherine's death in 1796 her son Paul ascended the throne. Paul despised his mother, and sought to undo much of what she had accomplished. His policies, however, were neither coherent nor effective. He fought the French at the time of the Directory (1798), yet in 1801 he planned a joint expedition with Napoleon whose purpose was the conquest of India. He first took steps to alleviate the work of the serfs (by limiting the work week), then effectively enserfed many formerly free peasants. Paul died at the hands of conspirators in 1801.

The three passages in this section are taken from the memoirs of Prince Adam Czartoryski, a prominent contemporary Polish statesman in the service of the Russian imperial court. The first passage is a description of the sumptuous coronation of Paul, and it emphasizes how important ceremonial was to the emperor. Our second passage in this section underscores Paul's interest in ceremonial, and is an account of the style of Paul's court. The third passage is an account of the murder of Paul, and a discussion of the implications of the assassination for European politics (translated by Adam Gielgud).

✥ *Paul's Coronation*[1]

In the beginning of the spring of 1797 the Emperor went to Moscow for his coronation. All the society of St. Petersburg followed him. It was still very cold, and the *habitués* of the salons of St. Petersburg were to be seen passing each other on the roads, wrapped up in furs and reclining in sledges, all hastening to the ancient capital of the Empire.

The ancient residence of the Muscovite Grand-Dukes, full of old associations, was the place where the ceremony of coronation was to be performed. It lasted several days. Paul had stopped for the night outside the barriers of the town, and made his solemn entry into the Kremlin on the following day, with an immense suite. He first went to the cathedral, where Plato, Archbishop of Moscow, who was regarded as the ablest and most learned prelate of the Russian Church, complimented the Emperor in biblical language. Then took place the coronation, the return to the palace with the same solemnity, and finally the Imperial banquet, at which the sovereigns and their families were served on a raised platform and under a magnificent canopy by the high officers of the Crown. Various minor ceremonies took place during the following days. The Emperor appeared in them all; he was passionately fond of display, and was proud of his figure and his grace. Whenever he appeared in public he walked with a measured step, and tried to look tall and majestic, though he was really short; it was only when he entered his apartments that he showed the fatigue which his efforts had cost him.

Each ceremony was preceded by a dress rehearsal, in order that everybody should know where to place himself and what to do. My brother and myself of course had to take part in the ceremonies as aides-de-camp to the Grand-Dukes. The Emperor was as active and busy as a stage manager, and looked after the smallest details of costume and decoration. He liked to appear to the best advantage before the ladies, and once he stood at the head of his favourite battalion of the Guard with a halbert, to do honour to the Empress, whom he had crowned with his own hand.

Paul ordered the King of Poland to follow him to Moscow, and insisted on his being present at all the solemnities of the coronation. He had to join the brilliant suite which surrounded the Emperor and his family—a sad part for a King to play. During divine service and the ceremonies which preceded the coronation, and were very long and tedious, Stanislas Augustus was so tired out that he sat down in the tribune which had been assigned to him. Paul at once

---

1. Reprinted from Adam Gielgud, ed. *Memoirs of Prince Adam Czartoryski and His Correspondence with Alexander I* (London, Remington and Company, 1888), v. 2, pp. 157–161.

Photo: The Kremlin Skyline, Moscow.

remarked this, and sent a messenger to tell him to stand up so long as they remained in the church; and the poor King had no alternative but to submit.

When the ceremonies were over, the Emperor and his family left the Kremlin to go to a more spacious residence, called the Petrovski Palace, in another quarter of the town. He gave up the rest of his time at Moscow to fêtes, parades, and military exercises.

There were fireworks and public banquets both at Moscow and at St. Petersburg, and the nobility gave the Emperor a ball in a vast hall where they usually met. These fêtes were somewhat tedious, and did not give satisfaction either to Paul or to his hosts. Numerous deputations from all the provinces of the empire were ordered to salute the Emperor and present addresses of submission. The delegates from the Polish provinces had an air of great constraint and depression. All of them had been citizens of an independent Poland; all had distinguished themselves either in their palatinates, at the last Diet, or in appointments of State. They saw their King relegated to a side gallery, and had to pass him to kneel before a foreign prince and declare themselves his subjects. I met several of my acquaintances, but could not feel any pleasure at seeing them again under such circumstances. I was struck by the change in their appearance; they looked confused and humiliated. Among the delegates from Lithuania was Bukaty, who had for several years occupied the post of Polish Minister in England. He was a man of simple manners and great good sense, and had acquired the esteem of the English people and their Government. Several of his English friends gave as a token of their friendship their names to his children at their christening. I had often dined with him in London with my mother. He was at that time stout, in good health, and in excellent spirits. He was now thin, his face was pale and haggard, his clothes, which in England fitted tight to his body, now hung about him in loose folds; he walked with bent head and an uncertain step—he was a picture of what Poland had become.

✢ *Formalities at Paul's Court*[1]

Both at Court and at parade the Emperor wished to establish strict exactitude in the ceremonies, in the way of approaching him and the Empress, and in the number and kind of salutations to be made. The Grand-Master of the Ceremonies, Natouyeff, treated the courtiers like recruits who do not yet

---

1. Reprinted from Adam Gielgud, ed. *Memoirs of Prince Adam Czartoryski and His Correspondence with Alexander I* (London, Remington and Company, 1888), v. 2, p. 155.

know their drill and in what order they ought to march. Whenever they met the Emperor they had first to make a profound bow, and then, with one knee on the ground, apply a sounding kiss to the Emperor's hand while he kissed them on the cheek. The same genuflexion had to take place when they approached the Empress, after which they had to withdraw without turning their backs, which often caused confusion, as they trod on the toes of the other courtiers who were coming forward to perform the same ceremony. Thanks to the efforts of the Grand-Master of the Ceremonies, the courtiers at length learnt to go through this manoeuvre without a hitch, and Paul, satisfied at the look of fear and submission which he saw on their faces, then made the etiquette less rigid.

✣ *The Assassination of Paul*[1]

At the Zuboff's house the guests had become so convivial that time went fast. At midnight the conspirators set out for the Emperor's palace. The leaders had drunk but moderately, wishing to keep their heads clear, but the majority of those who followed them were more or less intoxicated; some could even hardly keep their legs. They were divided into two bands, each composed of some sixty Generals and other officers. The two Zuboffs and General Bennigsen were at the head of the first band, which was to go to the palace direct; the second was to enter through the garden, and was under the command of Pahlen. The aide-de-camp in waiting, who knew all the doors and passages of the palace, as he was daily on duty there, guided the first band with a dark lantern to the entrance of the Emperor's dressing-room, which adjoined his bedroom. A young valet who was on duty stopped the conspirators and cried out that rebels were coming to murder the Emperor. He was wounded in the struggle which ensued, and rendered incapable of further resistance. His cries waked the Emperor, who got out of bed and ran to a door which communicated with the Empress's apartments and was hidden by a large curtain. Unfortunately, in one of his fits of dislike for his wife, he had ordered the door to be locked; and the key was not in the lock, either because Paul had ordered it to be taken away or because his favourites, who were opposed to the Empress, had done so, fearing lest he should some day have a fancy to return to her. Meanwhile the conspirators were confused and terrified at the cries of Paul's faithful defender, the only one

---

1. Reprinted from Adam Gielgud, ed. *Memoirs of Prince Adam Czartoryski and His Correspondence with Alexander I* (London, Remington and Company, 1888), v. 2, pp. 221, 238–242.

he had at a moment of supreme danger when he believed in his omnipotence more than ever and was surrounded by a triple line of walls and guards. Zuboff, the chief of the band, lost heart and proposed to retire at once, but General Bennigsen (from whom I obtained some of these details) seized him by the arm and protested against such a dangerous step. 'What?' he said, 'You have brought us so far, and now you want to withdraw? We are too far advanced to follow your advice, which would ruin us all. The wine is drawn, it must be drunk. Let us march on.'

It was this Hanoverian that decided the Emperor's fate; he was one of those who had only that evening been informed of the conspiracy. He placed himself at the head of the band, and those who had most courage, or most hatred for Paul, were the first to follow him. They entered the Emperor's bedroom, went straight to his bed, and were much alarmed at not finding him there. They searched the room with a light, and at last discovered the unfortunate Paul hiding behind the folds of the curtain. They dragged him out in his shirt more dead than alive; the terror he had inspired was now repaid to him with usury. Fear had paralysed his senses and had deprived him of speech; his whole body shivered. He was placed on a chair before a desk. The long, thin, pale, and angular form of General Bennigsen, with his hat on his head and a drawn sword in his hand, must have seemed to him a terrible spectre. 'Sire,' said the General, 'you are my prisoner, and have ceased to reign; you will now at once write and sign a deed of abdication in favour of the Grand-Duke Alexander.' Paul was still unable to speak, and a pen was put in his hand. Trembling and almost unconscious, he was about to obey, when more cries were heard. General Bennigsen then left the room, as he has often assured me, to ascertain what these cries meant, and to take steps for securing the safety of the palace and of the Imperial family. He had only just gone out at the door when a terrible scene began. The unfortunate Paul remained alone with men who were maddened by a furious hatred of him, owing to the numerous acts of persecution and injustice they had suffered at his hands, and it appears that several of them decided to assassinate him, perhaps without the knowledge of the leaders or at least without their formal consent. The catastrophe, which in such a case was, in a country like Russia, almost inevitable, was doubtless hastened by the cries above referred to, which alarmed the conspirators for their own safety. Count Nicholas Zuboff, a man of herculean proportions, was said to be the first that placed his hand on his sovereign, and thereby broke the spell of imperial authority which still surrounded him. The others now saw in Paul nothing but a monster, a tyrant, an implacable enemy—and his abject submission, instead of disarming them, rendered him despicable and ridiculous as well as odious in their eyes.

One of the conspirators took off his official scarf and tied it round the Emperor's throat. Paul struggled, the approach of death restoring him to strength and speech. He set free one of his hands and thrust it between the scarf and his throat, crying out for air. Just then he perceived a red uniform, which was at that time worn by the officers of the cavalry guard, and thinking that one of the assassins was his son Constantine, who was a colonel of that regiment, he exclaimed: 'Mercy, your Highness, mercy! Some air, for God's sake!' But the conspirators seized the hand with which he was striving to prolong his life, and furiously tugged at both ends of the scarf. The unhappy Emperor had already breathed his last, and yet they tightened the knot and dragged along the dead body, striking it with their hands and feet. The cowards who until then had held aloof, surpassed in atrocity those who had done the deed. Just at that time General Bennigsen returned. I do not know whether he was sincerely grieved at what happened in his absence; all he did was to stop the further desecration of the Emperor's body.

Meanwhile the cry 'Paul is dead!' was heard by the other conspirators, and filled them with a joy that deprived them of all sentiment of decency and dignity. They wandered tumultuously about the corridors and rooms of the palace, boasting to each other of their prowess; many of them found means of adding to the intoxication of the supper by breaking into the wine cellars and drinking to the Emperor's death.

The news of the death of the Emperor Paul suddenly fell upon us like a clap of thunder in a summer sky. The first result of the unexpected news was astonishment accompanied by a sort of fear, but these sentiments were soon followed by others of joy and relief. Paul had never been loved even by those whom he had benefited. He was too fantastic and capricious; no one could ever rely upon him.

PART TWO

❖

Russian History
in the
Nineteenth
and Early
Twentieth Centuries

Photo: Traditional Russian landscape with village rooftops.

Photo: The Kura River and the Caucasus Mountains in Georgia.

CHAPTER FIVE
*Alexander I: Reform and
the Napoleonic Invasion*

CHAPTER SIX
*Nicholas I: Reactionary Rule
and the Crimean War*

CHAPTER SEVEN
Alexander II and Emancipation

CHAPTER EIGHT
*Alexander II and the Rise
of Russian Radicalism*

CHAPTER NINE
*Nicholas II and the Twilight
of Imperial Russia*

ALEXANDER I: REFORM AND THE NAPOLEONIC INVASION

The rule of primogeniture had been established for the dynasty by Paul, and so his eldest son Alexander succeeded him in 1801. Alexander's reign (1801–25) can be divided into two distinct periods, the first, liberal, and the second, reactionary, with the Napoleonic invasion of Russia in 1812 serving as the dividing line between these two halves. His Swiss tutor La Harpe helped instill in the young Alexander the ideals of the Enlightenment, and the early liberal phase of his reign is characterized by an attempt to institute wide-ranging reforms in the Russian government. During this liberal phase, Alexander also granted a measure of toleration to religious minorities, abolished judicial torture, made it easier for landowners to free serfs (only one-half of one percent were actually freed), and allowed for greater freedom of the press (the number of printing presses in Russia went up at this time, as did the number of foreign journals imported into the empire). Many internal improvements were initiated by Alexander, as well, such as the construction of new canals and roads. Alexander was also interested in higher education, and he founded several new universities. In addition, he founded the first Ministry of Education in all of Europe.

The Ministry of Education was only one of several ministries established by Alexander in 1804, which were designed to replace the colleges which had been created by Peter the Great. The Senate was given increased powers in 1802, and Alexander's assistant, Mikhail Speranskii, drafted a plan for a new constitution and a national Duma, to be created out of local and regional dumas. Speranskii also proposed the formation of a Council of State, to be headed by Alexander, whose purpose would be to address various problems which arose within the empire. Although the constitution was never implemented by Alexander, he did form the Council of State and gather prominent liberals from throughout the empire to join an unofficial cabinet, sometimes referred to as the "Kitchen Cabinet" because it met informally in his kitchen. Alexander called it the "Committee of Public Safety" after the French revolutionary body of the same name. Its members represented the various ethnic groups and regions of the empire: Stroganov was from Russia; Czartoyski from Poland, Kochubey from the Ukraine, and No-vosiltsev from the Caucasus.

Alexander's foreign policy during the first half of his reign was primarily concerned with containing the French Empire led by Napoleon Bonaparte. Despite his sympathies with the French Revolution and its ideals, Alexander joined the War of the Third Coalition against Napoleon in 1805. Two deci-sive French victories in 1805 (Austerlitz) and 1807 (Friedland) brought Na-poleon's forces to Prussia and Poland. Alexander then removed Russia from the war in the Treaty of Tilsit in 1807, and agreed to participate in the economic sanctions of the Continental System against Britain. Hostilities re-sumed, however, in 1812 when Napoleon used the resumption of Russo-Brit-ish trade as an excuse for his invasion of the Russian Empire. Napoleon's Grand Armée *marched into Russia in June of that year and fought two im-portant battles with Russian forces commanded by General Mikhail Kutuzov at Smolensk (August) and Borodino (September). Following the Battle of Borodino, Kutuzov retreated and led a war of attrition, drawing the French farther into Russia and overextending the* Grand Armée's *lines of supply and communication (although some historians claim that there may have been no notion of a strategy of retreat). Napoleon captured Moscow, but the city soon burned and the French began a retreat in mid-October because of the loss of a safe winter base for the army. On the retreat along the road from Moscow to Smolensk, the* Grand Armée *suffered enormous casualties at the hands of Cossacks and civilian partisans, and it was virtually annihilated while crossing the Berezina River. Kutuzov followed the French across Europe, and joined with Austrian and Prussian forces to decisively defeat the* Grand Armée *near Leipzig in 1813. Paris was captured and the Bourbon dynasty was subsequently restored. While promoting the concept of Legiti-macy with other conservative Western political leaders (such as Prince Met-ternich) abroad in the Congress System, Alexander began a conservative phase of his reign within the empire. Many of the domestic policies initiated by Alexander in this reactionary period alienated the intelligentsia from the regime, and set the stage for the emergence of revolutionary organizations which aimed at changing or toppling the tsarist government. Political clubs, for example, were banned (and thus forced underground), and the govern-ment set and closely regulated the curriculum at Russian universities.*

Alexander died suddenly on December 1, 1825. He had not produced an heir, and the court was in a state of turmoil for three weeks before Alexan-der's youngest brother Nicholas assumed control over the throne (see next chapter).

Our first nine passages are taken from the memoirs of two keen Polish observers of Alexander's Russia: the courtier Madame La Comtesse Choiseul-Gouffier (translated by Mary Bernice Patterson) and the statesman Prince Adam Czartoryski (translated by Adam Gielgud). These are: Alexan-der's education (Choiseul-Gouffier), Alexander's plans of reform and the ministries (Czartoryski), the Ministry of Public Instruction (Czartoryski), the

Unofficial Committee (Czartoryski), Alexander's disillusionment with Napoleon (Choiseul-Gouffier), the suffering of the people wrought by Napoleon's invasion (Choiseul-Gouffier), Alexander's address to his troops on the Rhine (Choiseul-Gouffier), Alexander's address to the aldermen of the City of Paris (Choiseul-Gouffier), and Alexander's proclamation upon entering Paris (Choiseul-Gouffier).

The eleventh passage is an excerpt from Napoleon's Russian Campaign *by one of Napoleon's* aides-de-camp, *Count Philippe-Paul de Ségur, on General Kutuzov (translated by J. David Townshend). Our twelfth and thirteenth passages are taken from The London Times, and are examples of the British opinion regarding the conduct of the Russian people during the French invasion.*

Our final passage is an excerpt from Nicholas M. Karamzin's Memoir on Ancient and Modern Russia. *Karamzin (1766–1826) was the most prominent conservative Russian intellectual of his day. The* Memoir *was presented to Alexander in 1811 as an attempt to persuade the emperor to abandon his plans to reform Russian government and society. Ironically, Alexander did indeed abandon his plans for reform, but he was persuaded rather by his disillusionment with the ideals of the Enlightenment when Napoleon invaded Russia in 1812 (Napoleon was ostensibly exporting the liberal and revolutionary ideas of the French Revolution abroad).*

✢ Alexander's Education[1]

However, the choice which the empress made in the person of Colonel La Harpe as preceptor of the young duke, was calculated to calm maternal solicitude and satisfy the expectations of the nation. The wise instructor found in the august pupil confided to his care the happiest natural gifts. To perfect the work of nature and to accomplish the task committed to him, he endeavored to cultivate and develop the amiable and charming disposition of his young pupil.

Possessed of a warm and affectionate heart, Alexander conceived a devoted attachment for this estimable man, who had consecrated his time and care to him, and he always regarded his instructor as a sure and faithful friend.

Alexander loved to learn. He had a remarkable memory and quick, penetrating, and refined perceptions. In his early years he showed a taste for military science, occupying himself zealously with what he was pleased to call his service, following exactly and observing punctually the strictest discipline and subordination. He possessed in a high degree the love of order and work. That which one could not help most admiring in him was the perfect evenness of his temper, a quality very rare and very valuable in a sovereign, which had for its source the goodness of his heart. Nothing could change the sweet benevolence which showed itself in his face as well as in his actions.

Alexander spoke several languages, especially French, with elegance and fluency.

---

1. Reprinted from Mary Bernice Patterson, trans. *Historical Memoirs of the Emperor Alexander I and the Court of Russia by Madame La Comtesse De Choiseul-Gouffier* (Chicago, A. C. McClurg and Company, 1990), pp. 24–25.

✢ Alexander's Plans of Reform and the Ministries[1]

At length the Emperor's vague and floating ideas were consolidated into a practical shape. All the eccentric views which were mere fireworks were abandoned, and Alexander had to restrict his wishes to the realities and pos-

---

Photo: The stone gate in Moscow through which Napolean Bonparte is said to have entered the Kremlin.

sibilities of the moment. He consoled himself by indulging in his hours of leisure, which were daily becoming more rare, in hopes of progress which enabled him not to give up entirely the dreams of his youth. These dreams seemed to me like a tree transplanted into a dry and arid soil and deprived of its exuberant vegetation, whose despoiled trunk puts forth a few weak branches and then perishes. The Emperor's first step was to issue an ukase or manifesto to restore the authority and dignity of the Senate; this was a prudent course, calculated to predispose the public for the changes which were to follow. In speaking of the Senate he spoke a language which the Russians understood and which flattered the nobility; it was already the Supreme Court of Justice and Administration, for although every order of the Emperor, whether written or spoken, had the force of law, they had (especially those relating to general administration and the civil and criminal law) all to be addressed to the Senate, which was entrusted with the task of publishing them and seeing to their due execution. The various departments of the Senate were charged not only with trying on final appeal the civil and criminal cases of the empire, but also with punishing contraventions of the administrative regulations. It had the right of issuing ukases of its own founded on those of the Emperor, and when necessary, explaining and developing them; and it presented him with reports for his approval. The governors and financial authorities of the provinces were under its direct supervision, and it was their duty to send to the Senate regular and formal reports upon which the sovereign gave such orders as he pleased. It was accordingly called 'The Senate administering the Empire.' Its vague functions, partly judicial and partly executive, were not in accordance with modern ideas, being so cumbrous in form that they retarded and might even embarrass the course of government; but there was no way of touching this ancient organisation without exposing internal affairs to even greater confusion, as the institution of the Senate had become part of the routine and the habits of the government machine. The Senate was consequently allowed to retain its administrative functions, though it was intended to let them fall by degrees into desuetude. All its powers were confirmed in pompous terms of which the author was Vorontzoff, and to them was added the right of making representations on the Emperor's ukases. It was at the same time laid down that all the Ministers should make detailed reports of their functions, which the Emperor should send to the Senate for its opinion.

After laying the first stone of the edifice of the regulated legislative power, and devising a limit to the autocratic power, the Emperor turned his attention to the organisation of his government, so as to make its action more enlightened, more just, and more methodical. The government machine was irregular and intermittent in its action, and the administration was a

1. Reprinted from Adam Gielgud, ed. *Memoirs of Prince Adam Czartoryski and His Correspondence with Alexander I* (London, Remington and Company, 1888), v. 2, pp. 291–293, 294, 296–297, 302–304.

chaos in which nothing was regulated or clearly defined. The only administrative authorities that were recognised were the Senate and the Committees of War, of the Navy, and of Foreign Affairs. These were not deliberative or consultative bodies; one of the members of each committee, usually the president, brought the reports of the committee to the sovereign and then informed it of his decisions.

Russia therefore had reason to be grateful to the Emperor Alexander and those whose advice he then followed for having sought to introduce more order and method in the Imperial administration.

The object of the reform was to establish a system somewhat similar to those adopted in most other European States by separating the departments, defining their limits, assembling in each department matters of the same kind, centralising their management, and thereby augmenting the responsibility of the principal functionaries of State. It was hoped among other things that this would be an efficacious means of checking the numberless abuses and frauds which are the curse of Russia. The Emperor accordingly created for the first time Ministries of the Interior and of Police, of Finance, of Justice, of Public Instruction, of Commerce, of Foreign Affairs, of War, and of the Navy. As to the War Department, Alexander continued the system adopted by his father, insisting that everything relating to the army, down to the smallest appointment, should emanate direct from the sovereign, and that the army should know it.

Count Paul Strogonoff was at his request appointed assistant to the Minister of the Interior, and Novosiltzoff obtained the post of assistant to the Minister of Justice, retaining his former appointment of Secretary to the Emperor. This gave Novosiltzoff the most important place in the administration, as it was through him that the Emperor was to begin the work of reforming jurisprudence and the existing laws. He was well qualified for the task, as he had studied jurisprudence and political economy in England, and had made good use of the opportunities thereby afforded him of becoming conversant with those subjects. No one in Russia was at that time his superior in that administrative knowledge which was then only to be obtained by reading French and English works. His practical mind rejected all vain theories; he possessed skill and tact in dealing not only with individuals, but with the Russian public, which he knew thoroughly. He had bad qualities also; but these had not yet developed themselves. One of his greatest merits was that he seconded Alexander's wishes as to the improvement of the condition of the peasants, and he drew up the first ukase on this subject. He also reconstituted the commission for the revision of the law. This commission had been formed by the Empress Catherine, who thereby gained the flattering appreciation of Voltaire and the Diderots; but the only result was the publication of the philanthropic and philosophical instructions addressed by Catherine to the commission. It was dissolved soon after, and its proceeding were never made public. The new commission was organised by Novosiltzoff with the assistance of a German jurist, Baron Rosenkampf, on a vast and well-conceived plan. It was directed to codify all the existing Russian laws, which were very numerous and often contradicted each other, classifying them according to subjects, omitting such as were obsolete, and adding new ones when necessary, but taking care to retain in the new codes all that had entered for many years into the life of the Russian people, even if not quite reconcilable with the ideas of modern jurisprudence. The system adopted was somewhat similar to that of Justinian; but the task of the Russian codifiers was far more difficult than that of the Roman ones. The latter merely had to select and classify out of a somewhat confused mass of laws, most of which were admirable examples of wisdom and legislative science, while in Russia the laws were not only confused, but in many respects defective and insufficient. For such a work not only jurists, but real legislators were wanted. A similar code was to be prepared for the outlying provinces of the Empire, such as Livonia, Esthonia, Courland, and the Polish provinces of Little Russia, each of which had its own particular language, laws, and customs.

This great undertaking was begun methodically and pursued for some time with activity; Novosiltzoff was allowed by the Minister of Justice to make it his exclusive occupation. The classifications were prepared by Baron Rosenkampf, and so long as they were adhered to the work progressed; but it did not produce the results which were expected of it. This is usually the case in Russia; if there is no immediate result, the persons entrusted with the execution of the work are changed, and it has to be begun over again.

✣ *The Ministry of Public Instruction*[1]

The creation of a Ministry of Public Instruction was a remarkable innovation in Russia which was fruitful of great and salutary results, and posterity will owe gratitude both to Alexander and to the young men, then so much criticised, who supported him in his plans and gave them practical shape by dividing into special branches the confused organisation which was then in existence. Nothing could be more wretched or insufficient than public instruction in Russia up to the reign of Alexander. There was an Academy of Sciences at St. Petersburg which owed its only celebrity to the presence of some learned men whom the Government had brought to the Russian capital from abroad. Euler came when he was already an old man, and died there soon after. The transactions of this Academy were for the most part written

1. Reprinted from Adam Gielgud, ed. *Memoirs of Prince Adam Czartoryski and His Correspondence with Alexander I* (London, Remington and Company, 1888), v. 2, pp. 306–309.

in the French and German languages; it had no relations whatever with the country, and exercised no influence on its progress. At Moscow there was a university which was equally isolated, and was attended by not more than a hundred students maintained at the expense of the Government. The only other educational establishments in Russia proper were the so-called 'National Schools.' The teaching in these schools was bad and extremely meagre; the teachers were poor wretches whom idleness and *ennui* had rendered drunkards, and no respectable person sent his children to them. The establishment of the Ministry of Public Instruction completely changed all this. The existing universities of Moscow, Wilna, and Dorpat were better endowed, and three new ones were created—those at St. Petersburg, Kharkoff, and Kazan,—each forming an educational centre for a prescribed district, in which it directed all the educational arrangements. The University of Wilna was exclusively Polish, and during the next few years the whole of Russian Poland was covered with schools in which Polish feeling freely developed itself. This University, to which I appointed the most distinguished literary and scientific men of the country, and some eminent professors from abroad, directed the movement with admirable zeal and intelligence, and its consequences, which the Russians afterwards deeply regretted, seemed at that time to flow naturally from the Emperor's generous intentions with regard to the Poles. The University of Kazan was to look after the instruction of the Tartars and of Siberia generally. Each university had its curator, and the curators formed a council of public instruction, the President of which was the Minister. The persons appointed to these posts by the Emperor were such as to give a hope that the work of public instruction would be pushed forward with zeal and success. And in his capacity of curator he showed zeal and perseverance.

The universities which were most progressive were Wilna, Dorpat, and Kharkoff. The nobility of Livonia, Esthonia, and Courland did not look with favour upon the University of Dorpat, which had declared itself the protector of the peasants and the bourgeoisie.

✢ *The Unofficial Committee*[1]

We were privileged to dine with the Emperor without a previous invitation, and we used to meet two or three times a week. After coffee and a little conversation, the Emperor used to retire, and while the other guests left the

---

1. Reprinted from Adam Gielgud, ed. *Memoirs of Prince Adam Czartoryski and His Correspondence with Alexander I* (London, Remington and Company, 1888), v. 2, pp. 260–262.

palace, the four members of the Secret Council entered through a corridor into a little dressing-room, which was in direct communication with the private rooms of their Majesties, and there met the Emperor. Various plans of reform were debated; each member brought his ideas, and sometimes his work, and information which he had obtained as to what was passing in the existing administration and the abuses which he had observed. The Emperor freely expressed his thoughts and sentiments, and although the discussions at these meetings for a long time had no practical results, no useful reform was tried or carried out during Alexander's reign which did not originate in them. Meanwhile the Official Council, namely, the Senate and the Ministers, governed the country in the old way. Directly the Emperor left his dressing-room he came under the influence of the old Ministers, and could do nothing of what had been decided upon in the Secret Council; it was like a masonic lodge from which one entered the practical world.

This mysterious Council, which was not long concealed from the suspicions, or ultimately from the knowledge, of the Court, and was designated 'the young men's party,' grew impatient at not obtaining any result whatever from its deliberations; it pressed the Emperor to carry out the views he had expressed to us and the proposals he considered desirable and necessary. Once or twice an attempt was made to induce him to adopt energetic resolutions, to give orders and make himself obeyed, to dismiss certain superannuated officials who were a constant obstacle to every reform and to put young men in their place. But the Emperor's character inclined him to attain his end by compromises and concessions, and moreover he did not yet feel sufficiently master of the position to risk measures which he thought too violent. In our Council Strogonoff was the most ardent, Novosiltzoff the most prudent, Kotchoubey the most time-serving, and I the most disinterested, always striving to curb undue impatience. Those who urged the Emperor to take immediate and severe measures did not know him. Such a proposal always made him draw back, and was of a nature to diminish his confidence. But as he complained of his Ministers and did not like any of them, an attempt was made in the Council, before inducing him to change them, to discuss the matter in a practical spirit, apart from the abstract considerations of reform which had previously occupied us. Strogonoff accepted the post of Procurator of the First Department of the Senate; and Novosiltzoff was appointed one of the Emperor's secretaries, a place which gave him many advantages, as every letter addressed to the Emperor passed through his hands, and he had a right to publish the Emperor's ukases. His special department, however, was at first to deal with promoters of public undertakings, who are sometimes men of talent, but more often adventurers of very doubtful honesty who flock to Russia from abroad at the beginning of each new reign. This was a duty for which he was qualified by his varied knowledge in matters of finance and industry, and it was at the same time a school which did much to form his character. I must not here forget the fifth member of the Secret Council, M. de la Harpe, Alexander's tutor, who had come on a visit to his former pupil. He did not take part in the after dinner meetings, but he used to have private conversations with the Emperor, and frequently handed to him memoranda reviewing all the branches of the administration.

✥ Alexander's Disillusionment with Napoleon[1]

It would be difficult for me to say, from the different ideas thrown into the conversation, whether the Emperor Alexander then really desired the fall of Napoleon, or even believed that fall possible; but in speaking of Napoleon he repeated several times an expression which was very remarkable, *"The charm is broken."* Perhaps he thought only of that whose influence he himself had felt.

The Emperor Alexander said that in adopting revolutionary language the French had forgotten their own tongue. "It is very astonishing," added he, "but they no longer speak French."

1. Reprinted from Mary Bernice Patterson, trans. *Historical Memoirs of Emperor Alexander I and the Court of Russia by Madame La Comtesse De Choiseul-Gouffier* (Chicago, A. C. McClurg and Co., 1900) p. 151.

✥ The Suffering of the People Wrought by Napoleon's Invasion[1]

My father, having to give up to his Highness the Grand Duke Constantine the house which he occupied, changed his quarters and sent me to a country place not far from Vilna, to stay with friends. In going out of the town I was struck with the misery of the country people, whom privation of the absolute necessities of life by the interruption of trade, the bad harvests of the preceding year, and the continual passage of troops and transports had entirely ruined. The trades-people were obliged to furnish

1. Reprinted from Mary Bernice Patterson, trans. *Historical Memoirs of the Emperor Alexander I and the Court of Russia by Madame La Comtesse De Choiseul-Gouffier* (Chicago, A. C. McClurg and Company, 1900), p. 67.

the magazines of the army with provisions, and were paid in promises made in very uncertain terms. The evil, as is always the case, weighed most heavily on the poor. The peasants lost their horses, and even their cattle. This sad spectacle, I remember, put me in bad humor with the emperor, as if he had been the cause of the evils which are always the forerunners of war, not to speak of the plagues which are the inevitable followers of it.

❖ Alexander's Address to His Troops on the Rhine[1]

At the head of these united forces, and pursuing the remnant of the French army, ready to cross the Rhine, whose banks were covered with his triumphant ensigns, Alexander addressed his brave troops in a proclamation, of which a few passages will not be found out of place here, to show the great soul of the prince and the noble sentiments which governed him:—

> "Soldiers your valor has conducted you from the banks of the Oka to the Borders of the Rhine. . . . In invading our empire, the enemy whom we fight to-day has caused great disaster; but a terrible punishment has fallen on his own head. The vengeance of God has burst upon our enemies. Let us not imitate them, let us forget their deeds. Let us not carry hatred and vengeance into France, but a hand extended in token of peace. The glory of Russia is to conquer the enemy who attacks, and to treat as a brother the enemy who is vanquished. Our revered faith teaches us from the mouth of God to love our enemies and to do good to those who hate us. Soldiers, I am convinced that, by the moderation of your conduct in that hostile land which we are about to enter, you will conquer as much by generosity of conduct as by the force of arms, and that, uniting thus the valor of the soldier with the humanity of the Christian, you will put the seal to your great deeds, by preserving the renown which you have acquired of being a brave and enlightened people. I am also persuaded that your chiefs will neglect no means to keep our honor spotless."

---

1. Reprinted from Mary Bernice Patterson, trans. *Historical Memoirs of Emperor Alexander I and the Court of Russia by Madame La Comtesse de Choiseul-Gouffier* (Chicago, A. C. McClurg and Company, 1900), pp. 162–163.

✤ Alexander's Address to the Aldermen of the City of Paris[1]

On the thirtieth of March, the day memorable for Marshal Marmont's capitulation, the aldermen of the City of Paris repaired to the headquarters of the Emperor of Russia, and were admitted to an audience with the prince, who addressed them in the following kind words:—

"It is not against France that we are making war, but against the man who, calling himself our friend, our ally, has betrayed us three times; who has come to attack and ravage our dominions, and has left there traces of his passage which time only can efface. I love the French, and I recognize as enemy among them only Napoleon. Paris can count on my protection. Only the picked of our troops shall enter within the walls of this city.

"I will return good for evil. France needs a stable government which can assure her own repose and that of Europe."

Delighted with their reception, the aldermen carried back to Paris the kind and pacific words of the conqueror and friend of the French.

---

1. Reprinted from Mary Bernice Peterson, trans. *Historical Memoirs of Emperor Alexander I and the Court of Russia by Madame La Commtesse de Choiseul-Goeffier* (Chicago, A. C. McClurg and Company, 1900), p. 166.

✤ Alexander's Proclamation Upon Entering Paris[1]

On the day of his entry to Paris, Alexander published the following proclamation:—

> The armies of the allied Powers have occupied the capital of France. The allied sovereigns respect the wishes of the French nation. They declare that if the conditions of peace are to have the strongest guarantees the ambition of Bonaparte must be curbed; and the prospect for a lasting peace will be most

---

1. Reprinted from Mary Bernice Patterson, trans. *Historical Memoirs of Emperor Alexander I and the Court of Russia by Madame La Comtesse de Choiseul-Gouffier* (Chicago, A. C. McClurg and Company, 1900), p. 168.

hopeful when, by a return to a wise government, France herself offers the assurance of that peace. The sovereigns proclaim, therefore, that they will not treat with Napoleon Bonaparte or with any member of his family; that they respect the integrity of ancient France, such as she was under the legitimate kings. They can do even more, as they always profess the principle that, for the welfare of Europe, France must be great and strong, and they will recognize and guarantee that constitution which France shall adopt. They invite the senate, therefore, to form a provisionary government which shall provide for the needs of the administration and prepare a constitution which will be agreeable to the French people. The intentions which I have just expressed are shared by the other Powers.

Alexander.
Nesselrode.

Paris, March 31, 3 o'c. P.M.

✢ *Kutuzov, According to the French*[1]

He wanted to know everything about his new adversary. Kutuzov was described to him as an old man whose reputation dated from the time, long ago, when he had received an unusual wound. Since then he had always managed to take skillful advantage of events. Even the defeat at Austerlitz—which he had predicted—had increased his standing, and his last campaigns against the Turks had added to his stature. His courage was beyond question; but people reproached him with regulating its movements to suit his personal interests, for he calculated everything. His slow, vindictive, and crafty nature was characteristic of the Tartar, and he could prepare for implacable warfare with a policy of gentleness, flexibility, and patience.

On the whole he was a more able courtier than general. But he was a power to be reckoned with, because of his reputation and his ability to make everything and everybody contribute to it. He was able to please an entire nation and every individual citizen, from the general to the soldier.

Furthermore, in his outward appearance, his language, his clothing, his superstitious practices, there was much that reminded one of Suvarov—something of the ancient Muscovite, a strong national identity which endeared

---

1. Reprinted from J. David Townshend, trans. *Napoleon's Russian Campaign, by Count Philippe-Paul de Segur* (New York, Time Incorporated, 1965), pp. 53–54.

him to the Russians. In Moscow the people, completely carried away in their elation, kissed each other in the streets and believed that they were saved.

✤ *Alas, Poor Bounaparte*[1]

Alas, poor BOUNAPARTE! In what a labyrinth of blunders and contradictions dost thou wander! The facts are well known to be these—that the French were beaten in Russia because the war was a national one. The same spirit would have produced the same effect, whatever had been the form of the Government. The conflagration at Moscow, that splendid example of patriotic ardour, was the voluntary act of the inhabitants. The Russian Government had authorized its soldiers to set fire to some smaller places, such as Smolensko, but it would not venture on so great a sacrifice of the national wealth and dignity as the destruction of Moscow; and was totally ignorant of the means by which it was effected, insomuch as to be for a long time persuaded that it was the act of the French. Neither had Count Rastopchin any thing else to do with this noble act than to set the example of destroying his own house, and burnt it to the ground, together with the second library of the Russian Empire. For these facts we can vouch, on the authority of a Correspondent beyond all impeachment, and who was upon the spot.

To suppose that the Russian peasants could be induced to take part with their invaders, by a trumpery proclamation or two, only shows the same profound ignorance of human nature which BUONAPARTE had before displayed in Spain. A very slight perusal of the different Travels through that Empire would have taught him that the Russian peasant entertains the most exalted ideas of the national greatness, has the strongest feelings of patriotism, and the highest veneration for the Priests, the Nobles, and the Monarch. This the Corsican attorney's son should have known, before he sat up before a Regenerater—General of Empires; but the truth is, that in his blind and presumptuous confidence, he actually did issue proclamation, and form municipalities, and prate about the rights of man, till he found that he was wasting his breath on a race of beings far different from the supple and obsequious citizen-courtiers of the Thullieres, who are equally ready to swear allegiance to the Goddess of Liberty and to the King of Rome, and successively to profess a belief in the doctrines of the Catholic Church, the Alcoran, and the atoms of Epicurus.

---

1. Excerpt of a London Times editorial (Tuesday, December 29, 1812).

✤ *The Earl of Liverpool's Address*[1]

Amidst the many extraordinary events of the last twenty years, there were none more important, more singular, and perhaps unexpected, than those which have marked the last six months. We had beheld the greater part of Europe engaged in a combination against the Russian Empire. On this occasion, the Ruler of France had made the greatest possible efforts. Whether we considered the number or quality of the troops, and the ability and skill of the officers, it was evident that at no former time had equal exertions been made and which had for their object the total overthrow of the Russian Empire. At the commencement of the campaign in June last, the armies under the direction of the Ruler of France comprised a force of 350,000 men, accompanied by a body of 60,000 cavalry, and provided with everything necessary for conducting offensive operations on the most extensive scale. The numerical force of the Russian army was considerably below that of the enemy; and the late period at which the peace with Turkey took place, kept a large army in a remote part of the empire some time after the commencement of hostilities. Thus menaced with overwehlming numbers, the system of defensive warfare was resorted to by the Emperor Alexander, in conformity to the advice and opinion of our Great Commander in the Peninsula. Besides the nature and extent of the country there were reasons in the very composition of the Russian army which rendered this system advisable. Accordingly, we find that the Russians, though opposed to a cavalry so immense in point of numbers, yet retreated seven hundred miles unbroken; no corps were cut off, and no detatchment made prisoners, except such as might be taken in the field of battle; so that from the regular, patient, and scientific manner in which the retreat was conducted, there was good ground for hope, even looking to it alone, that the campaign would be ultimately successful. But the exertions of the Russian people were not less conspicuous than the valor of the troops. This was another of those wars in which, like that of the Peninsula, the people stood for something; and when we considered their devotedness to their country, their determination to sacrifice every thing for national independence, it was impossible not to feel sentiments of pride and exultation. If we looked at the evacuation and destruction of Moscow, what event was there in modern annals that could bear any comparison with it? Here was an ancient capital, containing a population of 250,000 persons, deserted and committed to the flames, that it might not afford shelter and an asylum to enemies of the country. (Hear, hear)

---

1. Excerpted from the Earl of Liverpool's Address to Parliament, published in the London Times (Saturday, December 19, 1812).

✤ *Karamzin's Conservative Vision*[1]

A commoner, dreading scorn even when he enjoys an eminent status, usually dislikes the gentry, and hopes with personal arrogance to make others forget his base origin. Virtue is rare. You must seek in the world common rather than superior souls. It is not my opinion, but that of all deep-thinking statesmen, that a monarchy is buttressed by firmly established rights of the well-born. Thus, I wish that Alexander would make it a rule to enhance the dignity of the gentry, whose splendor may be called a reflection of the Tsar's aureole. . . .

The gentry and the clergy, the Senate and the Synod as repositories of laws, over all—the sovereign, the only legislator, the autocratic source of authority—this is the foundation of the Russian monarchy. . . .

The day when we perceived clear skies over Europe, and Alexander enthroned over an *integral* Russia, we shall extol that good fortune of Alexander which he well deserves by virtue of his uncommon kindness!

Loving the fatherland, loving the monarch, I have spoken frankly. I now revert to the silence of a loyal subject with a pure heart, praying to God: may He protect the Tsar and the Russian Empire!

---

1. Reprinted from Richard Pipes, trans. *Karamzin's Memoir on Ancient and Modern Russia* (Cambridge, Mass., Harvard University Press, 1959), pp. 202, 204, 205.

Chapter Six

NICHOLAS I:
REACTIONARY RULE
AND
THE CRIMEAN WAR

*The problem of maintaining a legal, uninter-
rupted succession was not entirely solved when
Paul instituted primogeniture for the Russian throne. Many Russians, for instance, believed that Constantine, Alexander's eldest brother, would inherit
the throne in 1825. Constantine, however, was not interested in the throne
and in fact had secretly renounced his claim to it 1823. His marriage to a
non-noble Polish women in 1820 was unacceptable from a dynastic perspective, as their issue could not inherit the throne (and Constantine could not
convince his wife to convert to Russian Orthodoxy). Thus, his politically-
conservative younger brother Nicholas was in line to inherit the throne.
Many Russian liberals believed that Constantine was more amenable to their
plans for reform of the Russian government, including the adoption of a constitution for the empire. The upper- and middle-class reformers from northern Russia (led by Muraviev) who favored a constitutional monarchy joined
the reformers from the south (led by Pestel) who favored the creation of a
republic in openly supporting Constantine (Konstantin). They were collec-
tively referred to as Decembrists (after the month in which their movement
emerged.)*

*The Decembrists themselves were not a coherent group of revolutionaries.
In fact, the slogan "Constantine and Constitution" was not a revolutionary
expression, but could be presented as an attempt to assure the legality of the
succession according to primogeniture. The Decembrists utterly failed in
their attempt to educate the masses of their program. After Nicholas crushed
the movement, some army supporters of the Decembrist cause actually
stated, when questioned, that they believed Constantine to be the legitimate
heir and that Konstitutsia (i.e., "constitution," which has the feminine ending) was his wife. The movement was ultimately crushed when the army
swore allegiance to Nicholas on December 26, 1825.*

*Although a few reforms were made by Nicholas during his reign (1825–
56), such as an 1846–47 law calling for the emancipation of all serfs in
Russian Poland, he is most frequently depicted as a reactionary. Nicholas
did indeed wish to keep a watchful eye on the various ministries, and he
created his Chancery in order to do so. From the Chancery there emerged a*

form of political police, the Third Department, which sought to check the spread of revolutionary ideas from the West.

Nicholas strongly distrusted Western-oriented radicals such as Bakunin, Belinskii and Herzen. To counter these pernicious influences a veritable state ideology, called Official Nationality, was formulated by Count Sergei S. Uvarov and other reactionary thinkers. The Russian Orthodox Church was given privileges over all other faiths in the empire, autocratic tsarist rule was presented as the form of government most suitable for Russia, and attempts were made to Russify minorities (for example, by adopting the Cyrillic alphabet and Slavic names). As Minister of Education, Uvarov declared that the purpose of education was to prepare "loyal sons for the Orthodox Church, loyal subjects for the Tsar', and good and useful citizens for the fatherland."

This domestic policy had an impact on foreign policy during Nicholas' reign, in the form of a Pan-Slav and Pan-Orthodox stance with regard to Ottoman Turkish control over subject populations of Eastern Orthodox Slavs in the Balkans. The position manifested itself specifically in Russian assistance to the Greeks and Serbs in their respective struggles for independence (1829) and in the Crimean War (1854–56), in which the Russians sought to undermine Turkish power in the Black Sea and eastern Mediterranean region.

The British and French suspected Russian intentions after the conclusion of the Russo-Turkish Treaty of Unkiar-Skelessi in 1833. Fear of a "secret clause" in the treaty, which would give the Russians an unfair military and commercial advantage in the Middle East over budding British and French interests in the region, stirred up a great deal of anti-Russian propaganda in both Britain and France. At the Straits Convention (1841), the British and French governments both pledged support for the Turks in the event of a Russian attack on the Ottoman Empire. A conflict between Roman Catholic monks (supported by the French) and Greek Orthodox monks (supported by Nicholas) over control of the Christian shrines in Palestine in the 1850s became an international incident when Nicholas and Napoleon III of France tried to coerce the Ottoman sultan to favor one group over the other. The sultan, however, hesitated, and Nicholas then sent Russian troops into Moldavia and Wallachia (which had been under Russian protection since the Treaty of Adrianople in 1829). A great deal of anti-Russian propaganda again circulated in Britain and France when Russian ships sank Turkish vessels at Sinope Bay in 1853, and in the following year Britain and France declared war on Russia, beginning the Crimean War.

The principal theater of operation in the Crimean War was Sevastopol', a Russian city in the Crimean peninsula which was almost continuously besieged by British and French forces. It was to be easier for Britain and France to transport troops by sea to the front than it was for Nicholas to get his troops to the front on the poorly-maintained overland routes within his empire, and this proved to be the deciding factor in the war. The Treaty of

Paris was signed in 1856, ending the war, and freeing the straits from Russian control.

Our first, third, and sixth passages are taken from Edward Tracy Turnerelli's What I Know of the Late Emperor Nicholas and His Family, *published in London in 1855. Turnerelli resided in the Russian Empire for sixteen years, and the work is a memoir of his experiences. The passages which we have excerpted concern Grand Duke Constantine, the Decembrists, and the personal habits of Nicholas I. The second text is a letter from Nicholas to Constantine (dated December 13, 1825), translated by William Rae Wilson. Our fourth and fifth passages are taken from the writings of the Decembrists: a manifesto dated December 14, 1825, translated by Anatole G. Mazour; and the proclamation of the Southern Society, written by Serge I. Murav'ev-Apostol in an attempt to gain the support of soldiers who might be sympathetic to the Decembrist cause, translated by Marc Raeff.*

The seventh and eighth passages in this section are taken from Ivan Golovine's Russia Under the Autocrat Nicholas the First. *Although extremely critical of Nicholas and his governing style, Golovine offers important insights on Russian life in the 1840s, that can be compared to the reports made by Korb earlier in this volume concerning Russia during the reign of Peter the Great. The excerpts which we have selected are on Russian wildlife (a rather fanciful account) and the nobility of Russia.*

The subjects of our last four passages is the Crimean War. *The first of these is an account of the underlying conflict over the Christian shrines by a contemporary English observer, A. W. Kinglake. We next provide the text of Queen Victoria's message to the British House of Commons concerning the declaration of war, as preserved in the London Times (Tuesday, March 28, 1854). The use of an extensive system of trenches by the British and French in the siege of Sevastopol' anticipated the tactics on the Western Front in the First World War. The front line is described in our next passage by General Sir Edward Hamley. The Treaty of Paris is discussed by Hamley in our final passage.*

✤ *The Grand Duke Constantine*[1]

The education of the Grand-duke Constantine has been of a very superior kind. Persons connected with his studies have assured me that his love of study, assiduity, and perseverance were unbounded. He was always with a book in his hand even when a mere child; he speaks with facility and correctness several European languages. English he is perfectly familiar with; but his *grande passion* and *grande forte* is the Turkish. His profound knowledge of this language is the admiration of Orientalists, and in particular of those who have had the opportunity of conversing with him in this tongue. We are told, on this subject, that when he arrived, with his squadron, at Helsingfors, the very first person he invited on board of his vessel was—not the governor, nor the commandant of the town—but the professor of the Oriental languages attached to the university. The latter is said to have remarked:

"You would hardly believe that the Grand-duke is quite as proficient as I am in Turkish; he is acquainted with every manuscript the language can boast of, even with those least know to Orientalists. You would try in vain to puzzle him, either on a philological point, a political question, or upon any topic, material, financial, or social, relating to the past, present, or future probable state of the Ottoman Empire."

This predilection for the Turkish language, literature, and history, may have taken its first origin in the long-established belief which the Russians entertain, that a prince of their race is one day to possess Constantinople. The name which the Grand-duke bears may have contributed to increase this tendency, and to have inspired this prince with the hope that it is on him that the prophecy rests, which has been cherished by the Russians for upwards of 400 years, and of which everybody has heard.

---

1. Reprinted from Edward Tracy Turnerelli, *What I Know of the Late Emperor Nicholas and His Family* (London, Edward Churton, 1855), pp. 142–143.

Photo: Typical Conical dome of an Orthodox church in Georgia. The concept of Pan-Orthodoxy interested Nicholas I.

✤ Letter from Nicholas to Constantine (December 13, 1825)[1]

"Dear Brother,

"With heartfelt grief fully participating with Your Highness the deep affliction which has seized us both, I sought consolation in the thought, that in you, as the elder brother whom from my youth I have been accustomed to esteem and love from my soul, I should find a father and a sovereign.

"Your Highness, by your letter of Nov. 26. deprived me of that consolation; you forbade me to follow the emotions of my heart, and to fulfil that oath, which, although made to you not only from duty but from my internal feeling, you were not pleased to accept. But Your Highness cannot prohibit me from preserving feelings of attachment, and that internal oath which, having taken to you, I can never recall, and which on account of your love toward me, it will not be in your power to reject.

"The desires of Your Highness are fulfilled. I ascended to that station which you pointed out to me, and which you, although nominated according to the laws, declined to accept. Your will has been accomplished; but permit me to feel assured, that he who, contrary to my expectation and wish, has placed me on this very difficult road, will be on it my guide and conductor,—this duty you, in the presence of God, cannot refuse, cannot renounce; and to this power, to you, as the elder brother, entrusted by Providence himself, I shall deem it the greatest happiness in life to be always in subjection. With these feelings I conclude my letter. I beseech the Almighty that he may in his clemency preserve the life of Your Imperial Highness, which is so precious to me.

"Cordially you faithful subject,
"NICHOLAS.

"Dec. 13, 1825."

---

1. Reprinted from William Rae Wilson, *Travels in Russia* (London, Longman, Rees, Orme, Brown, and Green, 1828), v. 2, pp. 134–35.

✤ *The Decembrists and Their Appeal*[1]

Nicholas had many trials during his reign, but none so great and so cruel as that which occurred on the very day of his accession to the throne.

That day was indeed a terrible one—it was a day of conspiracy, insurrection, and massacre. So remarkable an epoch does it form in the life of the monarch, with whom we are at war, and so strongly did it portray two striking traits in his character, his courage and firmness, that I will describe it as briefly as possible.

After the death of Alexander, Constantine, the elder brother of Nicholas, assumed the reins of government, and was proclaimed Emperor.

The soldiers took their oath of allegiance to him.

But Constantine it seems, found the throne of the Tzars, (a rather perilous place even for the best of autocrats,) one which promised him neither rest nor safety; he was of a very violent temper, was feared and disliked by his nobles, and some took great pains to assume him that he ran a fair chance of being poisoned or of dying from some sudden apoplectic fit; and Constantine, believing such a result both possible and probable, after a very short reign, abdicated in favour of his younger brother, Nicholas.

The latter, little influenced by similar fears, accepted the dangerous post willingly and unhesitatingly, and called upon the soldiers of the Imperial Guard to take a fresh oath of allegiance to him.

The latter refused to obey his order, for a secret conspiracy had been formed to dethrone Nicholas, and establish a constitution in place of the absolute throne of the Tzars.

Prince Troubetskoi was at the head of the conspirators. He was to be dictator of the republic, and five talented, enthusiastic young men, Pestal, Rylaeff, (a poet) Mouravieff, Kahoffsky, and Bestoujeff, actively seconded his plans.

The conspirators, to induce the soldiers to act against Nicholas, persuaded them that the latter had usurped the throne, and that Constantine was immured in a dungeon and loaded with irons.

Thus, unfortunately for the cause they advocated, a lie was employed to forward their plans, and the blessing of Heaven could hardly be expected to accompany a project based upon falsehood.

It was found necessary to employ the same means to induce the soldiers to cry out for a constitution. As might be expected, the poor ignorant soldiers were not likely to understand the meaning of such a word; they were willing to have a republic, but not without an Emperor; they *must* have an Emperor—their intelligence could comprehend nothing else. This obstinacy at first disconcerted the conspirators; but, in order to render the affair somewhat more comprehensible, the soldiers were at last persuaded by their chiefs that *Constitutzia*, the Russian word for constitution, was the name of Constantine's wife. This was quite enough for the soldiers; and as they shouted forth by turns the cry of "Long live Constantine," and "Hurrah, Constitutzia," they all actually believed that they were cheering for the fair spouse of their imprisoned and ill-used Emperor.

---

1. Reprinted from Edward Tracy Turnerelli, *What I Know of the Late Emperor Nicholas and His Family* (London, Edward Churton, 1855), pp. 27–33.

This will give the English reader a tolerable idea of the way in which revolutions are effected in Russia.

The one I am alluding to broke out on the 25th of December, 1825, the very day, as I have said before, of Nicholas's accession to the throne.

About mid-day, news was brought to Nicholas that a portion of the soldiery was in full rebellion, and was preparing to march to the winter palace, the imperial residence of the Tzars, to wreak their vengeance on him and his family.

Nicholas, knowing the power the Russian clergy have over the minds of the people, sent the venerable Archbishop of St. Petersburg to expostulate with the rebels. The old man was scoffed at, insulted, and obliged, with his clergy, to take to flight.

Miloradovitch, the Governor-general of St. Petersburg, was now dispatched to summon the rebels to return to their duty. The only answer he received was a volley of bullets, which silenced his voice for ever.

The conjuncture was now a critical one. One moment more, and the throne might have been lost to Nicholas for ever—probably his life with it. Fortunately for him, he did not lose his presence of mind, but tearing himself from the embraces of his young wife, who is said to have dropped inanimate at his feet, he took his seat on his droschki, and drove straight into the very midst of the infuriated soldiers.

It is said that for a few moments he pronounced not a word, but looked with a calm and a bold eye around him.

A death-like silence succeeded to the furious cries and savage shouts which had been heard on the plain when he arrived.

Perceiving the effect his unexpected presence had created, Nicholas raising his hand aloft, exclaimed with a voice of thunder, "Soldiers, to your ranks."

They obeyed, as if under the influence of a charm.

"On your knees!" was the second order which burst from his lips.

Will it be believed? but it serves to show the power a Russian Tzar possesses over the minds of his people, even when under the influence of rebellious passions—that mass of armed soldiers, who had sworn death to Nicholas, awed by his look and voice, sunk prostrate in the dust before him, imploring his forgiveness.

All save one, who four times approached the Emperor with a loaded musket, with intent to shoot him; but four times the courage of the wretch failed, or the eye of Nicholas paralysed him, for he did not, could not fire.

With another portion of the troops, however, Nicholas was less fortunate. They refused to disperse, and the Emperor, as implacable in his anger, as he had proved himself firm and courageous, resolved to show them no mercy.

The artillery was ordered to advance and fire upon the insurgents.

Some even say, that the Grand Duke Michael, late brother to the Emperor, fired the first cannon, in order to urge on the hesitating gunners.

The havoc was dreadful—hundreds were mowed down by that terrible discharge of grape-shot. The rest submitted.

Several hundred are said to have been made prisoners.

Well, indeed, might Nicholas exclaim as he did, when he returned to his palace, "Good God! what a terrible commencement of a reign!"

Thus terminated that revolt—it established two firm convictions in the Russian people; first, that not only had Nicholas a bold, determined, courageous character, but that when called upon to chastise, he would shew himself severe and implacable.

✤ *Decembrists Manifesto Written by "Dictator" Trubetskoi (December 14, 1825)*[1]

The Manifesto of the Senate should proclaim:

1. abolition of the former government;
2. establishment of a Provisional Government until a permanent one is decided upon by representatives;
3. freedom of the press, hence abolition of censorship;
4. religious tolerance to all faiths;
5. abolition of the right to own men;
6. equality of all classes before the law . . .
7. announcement of rights for every citizen to occupy himself with whatever he wishes . . .
8. cancellation of poll tax and arrears;
9. abolition of monopolies on salt and alcohol . . .
10. abolition of recruiting and military colonies;
11. reduction of the term of military service for privates to be followed by equalization of military service of all classes;
12. retirement without exception of all privates who have served fifteen years;
13. the creation of Community, County, Gubernia, and Regional administrations; which are to be substituted for all civil service men appointed formerly by the government;
14. public trials;
15. introduction of a jury system in criminal and civil courts.

---

1. Reprinted from Anatole G. Mazour, *The First Russian Revolution* (Berkeley, University of California Press, 1937), pp. 283–284.

The Provisional Government is instructed to:

1. equalize all classes;
2. form all local, Community, County, Gubernia, and Regional administrations;
3. form a National Guard;
4. form a judicial branch with a jury;
5. equalize recruiting obligations among all classes;
6. abolish a permanent army;
7. establish a form of election of representatives to the Lower Chamber which will have to ratify the future form of Government.

✢ *Proclamation of the Southern Society, written by Serge Ivanovich Murav'ev-Apostol*[1]

God has taken pity on Russia. He has sent death to our tyrant. Christ has said: "Be no man's slaves, you who have been redeemed by my blood."[4] The world has not hearkened to His holy command and has fallen into an abyss of misery. But our sufferings have moved the Almighty—today He sends you freedom and salvation.

Brethren, let us repent of our long-lasting servility and let us swear that we shall have but one Tsar, Jesus Christ, in Heaven and on earth.

All the ministries of the Russian people have come from autocratic government. It has fallen. By the death of the tyrant God has manifested His will that we cast off the fetters of slavery contrary to Christian law. From now on Russia is free. But as true sons of the Church we shall not perpetrate any outrages and without internecine strife we shall establish a popular government based on God's law that says, "Let the first among you serve you."

The Russian army is approaching to reestablish a popular government derived from Christian principles, based on Holy Writ. No crimes will be committed. And thus, let our pious people remain at peace and in order, and implore the Almighty for the speedy conclusion of our sacred deed. Let the servants of the alter, until now left in poverty and neglect by our impious tyrant, pray God for us, as we restore the Lord's temples to all their splendor.

---

1. Reprinted from Marc Raeff, *The Decembrist Movement* (Englewood Cliff, N. J., Prentice-Hall, 1966), p. 123.

✤ *The Habits of Nicholas I*[1]

The Emperor Nicholas was in the habit of rising early in the morning, some even say at sunrise. He threw on an old grey military cloak which served him for a morning gown, and sat down at his writing-table in this costume, to prepare his orders for the ministers, generals, &c., who were to visit him in the course of the morning.

At eight o'clock, he dressed himself, and went out to take a walk on the Quay of the Court, along the banks of the Neva.

At nine o'clock he returned home to take his breakfast; at ten was ready to receive the different functionaries; between that hour and noon, he read and signed a multitude of papers; gave directions to the minister of war; the governor-general of St. Petersburg, &c., &c.

At one o'clock, his phaeton, droschki or sledge was at the door of his palace, and in it the Emperor took his place, and drove to visit some establishments in the capital; a hospital, barracks, &c. He arrived *à l'improviste,* entered by a back door, mounted the private stair-case, and woe to Monsieur le Directeur and his co-operators, if all was not in proper order; they remembered to their cost that unexpected visit of the Emperor Nicholas. Or he went to a review, attended at some religious or military ceremony, and as may well be imagined, there was always plenty of such business for his Majesty to attend to.

At three o'clock, almost daily, he might be seen walking down the Grande Morskaia, one of the principal streets of St. Petersburg, to pay a visit to the Grand-duchess Marie, his favourite daughter. In summer, dressed in a general's uniform of the Preobrajinsky guard, and in winter with the addition of a grey cloak wadded or lined with a light fur. As he passed on, every person stopped respectfully to bow to him, and stood till his Majesty had passed them, to which the Emperor replied with his usual military salute.

At five o'clock he sate down to dinner—and such a dinner! the plainest possible—the Emperor Nicholas was no epicure, no pamperer of his appetite—a simple dish of the common cabbage-soup, called *tschi,* the national dish of the peasants, a slice of the black bread, used by the lower classes, a glass of *qvass,* the sour national beverage, is what pleased Nicholas far better than dainty viands and *recherché* ragouts; and the former he generally partook of. No wine, or at least, very, very rarely—no smoking, for Nicholas detested the fumes of tobacco—in fact, a more abstemious man at his meals it would have been difficult to find in any country or any circle of society.

---

1. Reprinted from Edward Tracy Turnerelli, *What I Know of the Late Emperor Nicholas and His Family* (London, Edward Churton, 1855), pp. 22–26.

After dinner, immediately after, he retired to the boudoir of the Empress, and spent an hour or two with her and his family; his affection for the Empress is well known, but the full extent of it is known to few. When she was sick, the Emperor attended upon her himself, watched anxiously by her bedside, prepared and administered her food and medicines, and shewed her every care and attention that the most solicitous parent could shew to a favourite child. This affection for his suffering wife, was one of the most amiable traits in the Emperor's character.

In the evening, at a later hour, the Emporer went with or without the Empress to the theatre, circus, to a public ball or masquerade—he was particularly partial to the latter species of amusement. About midnight he returned home, often worked for a couple of hours before he retired to rest, then went to bed upon a hard horse-hair mattress, stretched upon a small iron bedstead, and got up the following morning to resume the routine thus described, which may be taken as the common mode in which the Emperor Nicholas passed every day of the year when he resided in the capital of his empire.

It is indeed but justice to say, that no man in Europe, priest or peasant, worked harder or more willingly than Nicholas. Nothing was done in his empire, but he examined ere it was commenced, even if he had not been the projector, as in five cases out of ten was the case. How one man could have sufficed for so immense a task, how one poor human head could have borne so monstrous a weight of of care and anxiety, has always been to me a matter of wonder. With such an accumulation of business to transact, such unceasing solicitude to combat with and such an awful responsibility to bear, (for every deed of ill that was done in Russia, was more or less laid at the door of Nicholas,) it was truly no sinecure to be an Emperor and Autocrat of all the Russias.

✣ *Russian Wildlife*[1]

Russia is very rich in game of every kind, and the chase is excessively easy; with the exception however of bear-hunting, which is as dangerous as it is diverting. This animal, which is peculiarly national, has very singular habits, with which the natives are perfectly acquainted. He is very fond of wheat, and often goes into the fields by night. The strawberry is his favorite fruit, and more than one woman has found herself face to face with a bear while

---

1. Reprinted from Ivan Golovine, *Russia Under the Autocrat, Nicholas the First* (London, Henry Colburn, 1846), v. 1, pp. 156–161.

gathering strawberries. A woman was once surprised at seeing a bear just opposite to her, she was excessively alarmed, and gave him a violent blow on the head with her basket. The beast, taken by surprise, was seized with a panic terror, and fled as fast as he could. It is said that he was found dead at some leagues' distant, and this is by no means improbable, for other facts of the same nature prove that this animal is subject to sudden terrors which are capable of causing his death.

In winter the bear covers himself with dry leaves, and remains lying on the same spot, sucking his paws, which in fact is all the nourishment he gets. A solitary peasant sometimes ventures to attack this animal, armed only with his hunting knife. He quietly allows him to place his front paws on his shoulders, in order the more easily to plunge the knife into his belly. At other times, two men go together, armed with forks, and seek out the bear in his retreat. They salute him in a friendly manner, call him by his name, Michael, and walk composedly for some way by his side. Suddenly, one of them makes a movement as if to attack the beast, which instantly falls upon him, leaving his side exposed to the other hunter, who plunges his fork into his loins, and with the assistance of his comrade easily overpowers him.

Sometimes the bear is taken by means of his defects, which are obstinacy and gluttony; snares of this kind are particularly successful with the cubs. Thus for instance, balls stuck with nails are thrown at them which they persist in endeavouring to crush, and the more pain the nails give them, the closer they drive them into their paws; or a barrel smeared with honey is thrown to them, which easily sticks fast to their head, and they are thus taken alive by the huntsman.

When the bear is wounded, he becomes furious, breaks the trees, or if there are none, tears up heaps of earth, which he tosses into the air. Whenever he throws down a man, he cleaves his skull, and consequently, if any one if so unfortunate as to be without defence, he takes care to fall before him in such a manner as to expose the less noble part of his body to the bear's claws.

Wolves are very common, in consequence of the want of regular battues, but in the western provinces, which are the most void of wood, they, as well as the bears, are becoming more and more scarce. They are inoffensive and timid in summer, but in winter they approach the dwellings and attack man and beast. They always fall upon the latter rather than upon the former, and above all, devour any of their own troop that are killed or wounded. The parts which they prefer, are the calves of men and the breasts of women. They are attracted by the squeaking of a pig, and whenever a peasant goes out to hunt them, he fastens sucking pigs to his traineaux, whose squeaking allures them.

The moorcock is the principal game in Russia, which it never leaves, and it is hunted both in winter and summer. In winter, a sort of tent of boughs is built in the forest, at the top of which the sportsmen place impaled cocks, that serve to attract the game. The habits of these birds deserve to be attentively studied. They have scouts which warn the band of the approach of the hunter, upon which they instantly flee away, but do not fly; they have leaders, which are the oldest and most experienced among them, and which it is extremely difficult to kill, for they are the last that suffer themselves to be caught in the trap of the impaled cock.

✢ *Golovine on The Nobility*[1]

There are two kinds of nobility in Russia—hereditary nobility and personal nobility. The first is acquired by the rank of officer in the army; in the civil service, down to the eighth class, which is equivalent to the rank of major. It may be conferred by the Emperor, and is also attached to certain orders that are bestowed on personal nobles or members of the clergy. Traders were excluded from this prerogative by the decree of the 30th of October, 1826.

Military officers, on passing into the civil service with a rank inferior to the eighth class, retain their rights of hereditary nobles.

Children born before the promotion of their father to the hereditary nobility are noble whenever the father acquires nobility by a rank or by an order. If he receives it by the favour of the Emperor, it must be specially indicated in the grant whether it is to extend to the children previously born. He whose father and grandfather have served, each for at least twenty years, in ranks which confer personal nobility, has a right to hereditary nobility.

The latter is divided into six degrees; 1stly, the nobles with the title of Prince, Count, and Baron; 2ndly, the ancient noble families; 3rdly, the military nobles; 4thly, the nobles of the eighth class; 5thly, the nobles of imperial creation; 6thly, foreign nobles.

Personal nobility is attached, in the civil service, to the ranks below the eighth class, or it is conferred by a nomination of the Emperor. The order of St. Stanislaus confers it on members of the Catholic clergy and on Baschkirs.

Of late years, the Emperor Nicholas, with a view to enhance the value of nobility, resolved not to confer it below the fifth class in the civil service; but, by limiting the service of the soldier to fifteen years in the guard, and that of the subaltern to twelve years, he has facilitated the access to the rank of officer, and consequently to hereditary nobility. The examinations of candidates, it is true, are conducted with greater strictness; but the liberty allowed them for a certain time to choose between the epaulette of officer and a pension of from 340 to 500 rubles per annum, has contributed not a little to discredit nobility.

---

1. Reprinted from Ivan Golovine, *Russia Under the Autocrat, Nicholas the First* (London, Henry Colburn, 1846), v. 2, pp. 1–3, 6–7, 20–21.

The noble cannot be deprived without trial of life, honour, or property: he must be tried by his *Peers**, and the sentence must be confirmed by the Emperor.

The noble is exempt from all corporal punishment before as well as during the trial, and cannot be subjected to it but for a fact posterior to that which has deprived him of nobility.

The crimes which entail the loss of his rights are treason, robbery, and murder.

The Russian noble is exempt from personal taxes and from the recruiting. His country-houses cannot be occupied by troops.

The hereditary noble has a right to establish on his estates any kind of fabric or manufacture; he may do the same in towns on inscribing himself in a guild. Upon the same condition he is allowed to carry on any sort of commerce.

He may acquire landed property with serfs, but he cannot possess serfs without having lands.

Emancipated serfs who have become hereditary nobles, cannot, before the third generation, acquire the lands on which they have themselves been inscribed as serfs; and, in case such an estate should devote to one of them by inheritance, it must be placed immediately under guardianship, or sold within six months.

With the exception of Tartars anciently settled in the country, none but Christians have a right to possess Christian serfs.

The Russian nobility is the head of the heart of the nation, nay, it is the entire nation; for, unhappily, it alone possesses rights, though illusory, while the rest of the people have nothing but obligations. It is in its ranks that the most civilized and the most distinguished men in every respect are to be found. Hitherto its only virtue was a patriotism which displayed itself as much in great sacrifices in the time of national wars, as by a blind devotedness to the throne, which it considers as the only guarantee of the public and private welfare. For it, liberty will necessarily be the first consequence and the immediate effect of the law of progression. So long ago as 1825, more than one hundred nobles sacrificed themselves for this sacred cause. Literature and the army are indebted to the nobility for their most illustrious characters. The Puschkins and the Karamsins, the Suworofs and the Kutusofs, were nobles before they became great authors and great captains. Upon the nobility then must rest the hope of the reforms necessary for Russia, for it is far less from it than from the Government that every obstacle to the development of the nation proceeds.

✤ *Background to the Crimean War:*
the Conflict over the Shrines[1]

But since it happened that, because of the manner in which the toll was levied, every one of the Holy Places was a distinct source of revenue, the prerogative of the Turks as owners of the ground was necessarily brought into play, and it rested with them to determine which of the rival Churches should have the control and usufruct of every holy shrine. Here, then, was a subject of lasting strife. So long as the Ottoman Empire was in its full strength, the authorities at Constantinople were governed in their decision by the common appliances of intrigue, and most chiefly, no doubt, by gold; but when the power of the Sultans so waned as to make it needful for them to contract engagements with Christian sovereigns, the monks of one or other of the Churches found means to get their suit upheld by foreign intervention. In 1740, France obtained from the Sultan a grant which had the force of a treaty, and its Articles, or 'Capitulations,' as they were sometimes called, purported to confirm and enlarge all the then existing privileges of the Latin Church in Palestine. But this success was not closely pursued, for in the course of the succeeding hundred years, the Greeks, keenly supported by Russia, obtained from the Turkish Government several firmans which granted them advantages in derogation of the treaty with France; and until the middle of this century France acquiesced.

In the contest now about to be raised between France and Russia, it would be wrong to suppose that, so far as concerned strength of motive and sincerity of purpose, there was any approach to an equality between the contending Governments. In the Greek Church the rite of pilgrimage is held to be of such deep import, that if a family can command the means of journeying to Palestine, even from the far-distant provinces of Russia, they can scarcely remain in the sensation of being truly devout without undertaking the holy enterprise; and to this end the fruits of parsimony and labour, enduring through all the best years of manhood, are joyfully devoted. The compassing of vast distances with the narrow means at the command of a peasant is not achieved without suffering so great as to destroy many lives. This danger does not deter the brave pious people of the North. As the reward of their sacrifices, their priests, speaking boldly in the name of Heaven, promise them ineffable blessings. The advantages held out are not understood to be dependent upon the volition and motive of the pilgrim, for they hold good, as baptism does, for children of tender years. Of course

---

1. Reprinted from Alexander W. Kinglake, *The Invasion of the Crimea* (London, William Blackwood and Sons, 1885), v. 1, pp. 43–50.

every man who thus came from afar to the Church of the Holy Sepulchre was the representative of many more who would do the like if they could. When the Emperor of Russia sought to gain or to keep for his Church the holy shrines of Palestine, he spoke on behalf of fifty millions of brave, pious, devoted subjects, of whom thousands for the sake of the cause would joyfully risk their lives. From the serf in his hut even up to the Great Czar himself, the faith professed was the faith really glowing in the heart, and violently swaying the will. It was the part of wise statesmen to treat with much deference an honest and pious desire which was rooted thus deep in the bosom of the Russian people.

On the other hand, the Latin Church seems not to have inculcated pilgrimage so earnestly as its Eastern rival. Whilst the Greek pilgrim-ships poured out upon the landing-place of Jaffa the multitudes of those who had survived the misery and the trials of the journey, the closest likeness of a pilgrim which the Latin Church could supply was often a mere French tourist, with a journal and a theory, and a plan of writing a book. It is true that the French Foreign Office had from time to time followed up those claims to protect the Latin Church in the East which had arisen in the times when the mistresses of 'the most Christian kings' were pious; but it was understood that by the course of her studies in the eighteenth century, France had obtained a tight control over her religious feelings. Whenever she put forward a claim in her character as 'the eldest daughter of the Church,' men treated her demand as political, and dealt with it accordingly; but as to the religious pretension on which it was based, Europe always met that with a smile. Yet it will presently be seen that a claim which tried the gravity of diplomatists might be used as a puissant engine of mischief.

There was repose in the empire of the Sultan, and even the rival Churches of Jerusalem were suffering each other to rest, when the French President, in cold blood, and under no new motive for action, took up the forgotten cause of the Latin Church of Jerusalem, and began to apply it as a wedge for sundering the peace of the world.

The French Ambassador at Constantinople was instructed to demand that the grants to the Latin Church which were contained in the treaty of 1740 should be strictly executed; and, since the firmans granted during the last century to the Greek Church were inconsistent with the capitulations of 1740, and had long been in actual operation, the effect of this demand on the part of the French President was to force the Sultan to disturb the existing state of repose, to annul the privileges which (with the acquiescence of France) the Greek Church had long been enjoying, to drive into frenzy the priesthood of the Greek Church, and to rouse to indignation of the Sovereign of the great military empire of the North, with all those millions of pious and devoted men who, so far as regarded this question, were heart and soul with their Czar. 'The Ambassador of France,' said our Foreign Secretary, was the first to disturb the *status quo* in which the matter rested. Not that 'the disputes of the Latin and Greek Churches were not very active, but that without some political action on the part of France, those quarrels would never have troubled the relations of friendly Powers. If report is to be believed, the French Ambassador was the first to speak of having recourse to force, and to threaten the intervention of a French fleet to enforce the demands of his country. We should deeply regret any dispute that might lead to conflict between two of the great Powers of Europe; but when we reflect that the quarrel is for exclusive privileges in a spot near which the heavenly host proclaimed peace on earth and goodwill towards men—when we see rival Churches contending for mastery in the very place where Christ died for mankind—the thought of such a spectacle is melancholy indeed. . . . Both parties ought to refrain from putting armies and fleets in motion for the purpose of making the tomb of Christ a cause of quarrel among Christians.'

Still, in a narrow and technical point of view, the claim of France might be upheld, because it was based upon a treaty between France and the Porte which could not be legally abrogated without the consent of the French Government; and the concessions to the Greek Church, though obtained at the instance of Russia, had not been put into the form of treaty engagements, and could always be revoked at the pleasure of the Sultan. Accordingly M. de Lavalette continued to press for the strict fulfillment of the treaty; and being guided, as it would seem, by violent instructions, and being also zealous and unskilled, he soon carried his urgency to the extremity of using offensive threats, and began to speak of what should be done by the French fleet. The Russian Envoy, better versed in affairs, used wiser but hardly less cogent words, requiring that the firmans should remain in force; and since no ingenuity could reconcile the engagements of the treaty with the grants contained in the firmans, the Porte, though having no interest of its own in the question, was tortured and alarmed by the contending negotiators. It seemed almost impossible to satisfy France without affronting the Emperor Nicholas.

The French, however, did not persist in claiming up to the very letter of the treaty of 1740, whilst on the other hand there were some of the powers of exclusion granted by the firmans which the Greeks could be persuaded to forego; and thus the subject remaining in dispute was narrowed down until it seemed almost too slender for the apprehension of laymen.

Stated in bare terms, the question was whether, for the purpose of passing through the building into their Grotto, the Latin monks should have the key of the chief door of the Church of Bethlehem, and also one of the keys of each of the two doors of the sacred Manger, and whether they should be at liberty to place in the sanctuary of the Nativity a silver star adorned with the arms of France. The Latins also claimed a privilege of worshipping once a-year at the shrine of the blessed Mary in the Church of Gethsemane, and they went on to assert their right to have a cupboard and a lamp in the tomb 'of the Virgin;' but in this last pretension they were not well supported by France; and, virtually, it was their claim to have a key of the great door of the Church of Bethlehem, instead of being put off with a key of the lesser door, which long remained insoluble, and had to be decided by the advance of armies and the threatening movement of fleets.

Diplomacy, somewhat startled at the nature of the question committed to its charge, but repressing the coarse emotion of surprise, 'ventured,' as it said, 'to inquire whether in this case a key meant an instrument for opening a door, only not to be employed in closing that door against Christians of other sects, or whether it was simply a key—an emblem;' but Diplomacy answered that the key was really a key—a key for opening a door; and its evil quality was—not that it kept the Greeks out, but that it let the Latins come in.

M. de Lavalette's demand was so urgently, so violently pressed, that the Porte at length gave way, and acknowledged the validity of the Latin claims in a formal note: but the paper had not been signed more than a few days when the Russian Minister, making hot remonstrance, caused the Porte to issue a firman, ratifying all the existing privileges of the Greeks, and virtually revoking the acknowledgment just given to the Latins. Thereupon, as was natural, the French Government became indignant, and to escape its anger the Porte promised to evade the public reading of the firman at Jerusalem; but the Russian Minister not relaxing his zeal, the Turkish Government secretly promised him that the Pasha of Jerusalem should be instructed to try to avoid giving up the key to the Latin monks.

✠ *Queen Victoria's Declaration of War*[1]

"Victoria Regina:—

"Her Majesty thinks it proper to acquaint the House of Commons that the negotiations in which Her Majesty, in concert with her allies, has for some time past been engaged with His Majesty the Emperor of All the Russias, have terminated, and that Her Majesty feels bound to afford active assistance to her ally the Sultan against unprovoked aggression.

"Her Majesty has given directions for laying before the House of Commons copies of such papers, in addition to those already communicated to Parliament, as will afford the fullest information with regard to the subject of these negotiations. It is a consolation to Her Majesty to reflect that no endeavours have been wanting on her part to preserve to her subjects the blessings of peace.

"Her Majesty's just expectations have been disappointed, and Her Majesty relies with confidence on the zeal and devotion of her faith/   ˉ m-

---

1. From The London Times, Tuesday, March 28, 1854.

mons, and on the exertions of her brave and loyal subjects, to support her in her determination to employ the power and resources of the nation for protecting the dominions of the Sultan against the encroachments of Russia.''

✤ The Horrors of the Front Line[1]

Simultaneously with the entry of the French works, 800 Russians moved out for an advance upon our Right Attack, but were easily repulsed for the time. This attack had been made on the part of the trenches next the Docks ravine. An hour later another assault (which apparently ought to have been in concert with the first) was made on the left portion of the same trenches by Greek and other volunteers. Led by an Albanian, in the dress of his country, they broke into the parallel, where the leader, first shooting one of our officers, discharged a pistol ineffectually at the magazine, and was then killed himself. The assailants moved along the trench from left to right till the guards and working parties, having been got together, met and drove them back upon the Redan.

At the same time with this last, another assault had been directed, with 500 men, on the advanced trench of our Left Attack, close to where the ridge was cut short by the ravine, and penetrated to the third parallel, where they were attacked by the nearest bodies of those guarding the trenches, and driven back like the rest. In these fights the officer commanding the guards of the Right Attack was wounded and captured, as was the engineer of the Left Attack, with about fifteen men, and a quantity of intrenching tools, dropped by the working parties when they took up their arms. In all, we lost seventy men. The enemy left about forty dead in front of our Right Attack, ten killed and two wounded in the trenches of the Left; and his losses, in all, that night were 1300 men.

If the Russians aimed, in this sortie, at establishing themselves in the French lines, it was so far a failure. But the object of such an enterprise is mostly in inflict hasty damage and discouragement on the enemy, and to gain a temporary facility for executing some of the defensive operations; and on this ground the Russians might claim a certain success, for in the following night they connected the pits in front of the Mamelon by a trench, which their engineer extended to the verge of the ravine. Thus he had succeeded in forming and occupying, within eighty yards of the French, an intrenched line, supported by, while it covered, the Mamelon.

---

1. Reprinted from General Sir Edward Hamley, *The War in the Crimea* (New York, Charles Scribner's Sons, 1891), pp. 200–203.

A truce was agreed on for burying the slain, to begin half-an-hour after noon on the 24th. White flags were then raised over the Mamelon and the French and English works, and many spectators streamed down the hillsides to the scene of contest. The French burial parties advanced from their trenches, and hundreds of Russians, some of them bearing stretchers, came out from behind the Mamelon. The soldiers of both armies intermingled on friendly terms. The Russians looked dirty and shabby, but healthy and well fed. Between these groups moved the burial parties, collecting the bodies and conveying them within the lines on both sides. At 450 yards from the scene rose the Mamelon, its parapet lined with spectators. Five hundred yards beyond it, separated by a level space, stood the Malakoff, its ruined tower surrounded by earthen batteries; and through the space between it and the Redan appeared the best built portion of the city, jutting out into the harbour, and near enough for the streets, with people walking in them, the marks of ruin from shot, the arrangement of the gardens, and the line of sunken ships, to be plainly visible. About forty bodies were removed from the front of the English Right Attack, among them that of the Albanian leader, partially stripped, and covered again with his white kilt and other drapery. In two hours the business was over, the soldiers on both sides had withdrawn within their lines, the flags were lowered, and the fire went on as before.

This was the only considerable attempt as yet made on the trenches, but small losses from fire occurred in them almost daily and nightly. At one time the men killed had been taken at night to the front of the works, and there buried, and a strange experience fell in consequence on a young engineer, destined to a place in the esteem of his country far beyond that of any other soldier of these latter generations, Charles Gordon. In carrying a new approach to the front, these graves lay directly across it, and he described how the working party had to cut their way straight through graves and occupants, and how great was the difficulty he found in keeping the men to their horrible task, which, however, was duly completed. He had a brother, Enderby Gordon, on the staff of the artillery, to whom he used to relate his experiences; among others, of strolls he was in the habit of taking at night far beyond our trenches, one of which led him up close to the outside of the Russian works, so that he could hear the voices of the men on the parapet. A singularly ghastly incident of these burials took place about this time. One night two men had carried the body of a comrade, just slain, on to the open ground for interment, and had finished digging the grave, and placing the body in it, when, as they were about to fill it in, a shot from the enemy, who had perhaps heard them at work, killed one of them. The survivor laid his comrade's body beside the other, buried both, and returned to the trench.

✤ *The Allies and the Treaty of Paris*[1]

The Treaty of Paris was signed on the 30th March. It was well known in the congress that, but for England, the conditions imposed on Russia would have been far easier. And though they were still too easy, yet England might congratulate herself on having obtained so much in circumstances so adverse. For the Emperor was perhaps the only man in France who held firmly to the alliance. The French nation had no strong interest in the affairs of Turkey, and was now ready to believe, and to proclaim, that it had been made the tool of England. And Louis Napoleon himself had already obtained from the war all that was necessary for his purpose, in the victory of the Tchernaya, and the brilliant finale of the Malakoff; while the unfortunate condition into which his army in the Crimea had fallen during the winter supplied an ample reason for desiring peace.

---

1. Reprinted from General Sir Edward Hamley, *The War in the Crimea* (New York, Charles Scribner's Sons, 1891), p. 301.

Chapter Seven

ALEXANDER II
AND EMANCIPATION

Nicholas I died near the end of the Crimean War (March 2, 1855). He was succeeded by his son Alexander, who capitulated to the British and French in 1856 following the fall of Sevastopol'. Believing Russia's defeat to have been caused by longstanding economic and social problems, Alexander II dedicated much of his reign (1855–81), to the attempt to modernize the empire by enacting a number of progressive reforms. The most significant problem facing Russia, Alexander felt, was the fact that Russian peasants were stifled by the institution of serfdom. The army, after all, was overwhelmingly comprised of peasants, and the stability of the empire could not long be maintained in the aftermath of a humiliating defeat in a war that was costly in a financial sense and especially in terms of the suffering experienced by the soldiers in the field. Without a drastic move to alleviate the plight of the serfs, the foundations of imperial government could potentially be shaken by the spread of revolutionary activity among the peasant population. Thus, on Sunday, March 3, 1861, the serfs were officially freed by an imperial manifesto read in all the Russian Orthodox churches within the empire.

According to the provisions of the imperial manifesto, however, the serfs were required to purchase their own land in a series of annual redemption payments. The economic hardships experienced by most peasants as a result of insufficient harvests precluded the successful completion of their payments, and many went into debt. The peasant commune (mir) was entrusted with the task of ensuring that payments would be made, but it proved unequal to the task. The general failure of agricultural reform coincided with officially-sanctioned industrialization projects within the empire. Many peasants now fled rural poverty to seek employment in the burgeoning industries located in the vicinity of Moscow and St. Petersburg, as well as in the Urals. Consequently, in this period of desperation in the agricultural sector a demographic shift occurred away from rural districts towards the urbanization areas of European Russia.

In this climate of agricultural failure, a number of reform groups emerged within the intelligentsia. Among the earliest of these groups were the Narodniks, whose name derives from the Russian word for "people" (i.e., peasants), narod. *The Narodniks were middle- and upper-class intellectuals who argued that the peasants should be freed from the cycle of redemption payments which were drawing increasing numbers of farmers into poverty. The Narodniks, however, also wanted the legalization of unions to protect the industrial workers from exploitation and abuse at the hands of factory owners; the creation of a European-style parliament so that social legislation might be enacted by representatives of the people; and a republican form of government.*

Many Narodniks argued that the Emancipation Manifesto was a fraudulent document, and that the solution to the growing agricultural problems in the empire was to use the mir *as the basis of a uniquely Russian form of peasant socialism. They believed the Russian peasants to be a natural revolutionary class, and thus many Narodniks began a program to educate the peasant population in the "Going to the People" movement, which occurred in the so-called "Mad Summer" of 1874. Thousands of university students left their studies in the summer of 1874 to educate the peasants out in the countryside. Ultimately, the "Going to the People" movement failed because of the fact that the peasants were unreceptive to the arguments put forth by the Narodniks. In particular, the peasants were loyal to the tsar', whom they called Tsar'—(beloved) father". According to the peasants, the landlords, rather than the tsar', were responsible for the hardships which they were experiencing.*

In addition to issuing the Emancipation Manifesto, Alexander called for a consultative assembly of liberals and conservatives whose purpose was governmental and financial reform in general. County councils (zemstvos) were created in an 1864 reorganization of local governmental structures within the empire, and municipal self-government was enhanced by an 1870 law established by Alexander. In 1874, a reform of the army also took place.

The pace of reform, however, was not rapid enough for certain radical groups which emerged after the failure of the Narodnik movement. Perhaps the most radical group was the People's Will, which advocated violence against the regime as a means of effecting change. To the horror of most Russian subjects, the People's Will succeeded in assassinating Alexander himself, on March 13, 1881.

The first passage in this section is a description of Alexander by Turnerelli. Our next passage is an 1856 description of the mir, *provided by Baron Von Haxthausen. An excerpt from Alexander's address to the nobles assembled in Moscow (march 30, 1856), concerning the necessity of emancipation, is our third selection (translated by Terence Emmons). The fourth passage is a summary of the Emancipation Manifesto. Our fifth and sixth passages are American views of Russian emancipation. Taken from Confederate and Union newspapers during the Civil War, they reveal as much about their audiences as they do about the Emancipation Manifesto. The Charleston Mercury, for example, attaches a great deal of significance to the liberation of a servile population of European laborers.*

The seventh passage is an excerpt from an address by Alexander to the nobles in 1863, concerning the need for further reform (translated by

Stephen Graham). Our eighth passage is taken from memoirs of Frederick Seward, and reports on the sale of Russian America to the United States. The ninth passage is an excerpt from the memoirs of Alexander Herzen addressing the emergence of organized opposition to the tsarist regime. Herzen spent half of his life in voluntary exile in the West, and was particularly active in London, publishing opposition journals there (such as The Polar Star *and* The Bell).

The Slavophile movement believed that the Slavic peoples in general and the Russians in particular had a preeminent role to play in human history. Among the early leaders of the movement were Khomiakov and Kireevskil, and after the Crimean War, the Aksakov brothers (Ivan and Constantine), were the most prominent figures in Slavophile circles. The Slavophiles (as well as the more militant Pan-Slavs) believed that the tsar represented the aspirations of the Russian people more clearly than any other person or institution in Russian history. Thus, when Alexander II was assassinated in 1881, many Slavophiles lamented greatly at the loss of the individual who embodied the greatness of the Russian nation. Our tenth passage is an excerpt from Ivan Aksakov's address to the St. Petersburg Benevolent Slav Society concerning the assassination of Alexander II (translated by Hans Kohn).

Our final passage is excerpted from the remarks made by a French diplomat at Alexander's funeral.

✠ *A Description of Alexander II*[1]

The present Emperor, Alexander II., is, at the period I write, about thirty-five years of age, and is certainly one of the most striking and interesting members of the imperial family of Russia.

While writing the short account I purpose giving of this prince, I cannot but recall to mind a little incident which relates to his boyhood, and which he himself must remember with pleasure and gratitude.

On that fatal day to which I have more than once alluded, the day of the Emperor's accession to the throne, at the very moment when Nicholas had torn himself from the embrace of his young bride, he took in his arms the young Grand-duke, at that time only eight years of age, and previous to leaving the Winter Palace to face the insurgents, he assembled around him his body-guard of the palace, ordered the men to load their guns and guard every avenue. He then gave the child into the hands of the soldiers, saying, "*Fellows,* I confide to you my son; I know you will defend him to the last if necessary," and with these words he rode away to meet death or triumph as might turn out.

"The Finnish Chasseurs," says an author who has written a life of the late Emperor, "were moved even to tears at this mark of his confidence; they took the boy in their arms, lavished upon him a thousand caresses, and swore that their bodies should be ramparts before him. It was a touching sight to behold the imperial child, delicate rather than robust, pale and of fair complexion, passed on from rank to rank, from one soldier to another, terrified perhaps by the caresses which these warlike men, now excited to the highest pitch, bestowed upon him. But he was in sure hands. When an act of confidence has touched the heart of the Russian soldier, and he has given his faith, he will be hewed to pieces rather than abandon his trust. The Chasseurs watched over their precious charge, and refused to surrender him even to his governor, Colonel Moerder, when he came to claim him.

"God knows the intention of all," they exclaimed; "but we will only surrender up the son of our father to our father himself in his own person."

The present Tzar inherits the beauty of his father and his fine majestic figure. His features, however, are not so regular as those of the late Emperor, but there is probably more of kindness and less of sternness in their expression.

---

1. Reprinted from Edward Tracy Turnerelli, *What I Know of the Late Emperor Nicholas and His Family* (London, Edward Churton, 1855), pp. 126–128.
Photo: Cathedral of Christ on the Blood, on the site of the assassination of Alexander II, in St. Petersburg.

✢ *Von Haxthausen on the Mir*[1]

As the educated classes have been alienated from the popular customs, of which they take a foreign view, confounding their national institutions with those in other countries, they have given to many words a foreign meaning, so that both in the language of common life, the sciences, and business, there is often no word which properly expresses the national idea. As an instance of this I will adduce the Russian word *Mir*. In all the countries of Western Europe an idea has been attached to the Latin word *Communitas*, and the German *Gemeinde*, which have only slight shades of difference; in each language the work has a precise signification, intelligibles both to the educated and uneducated classes. This is not the case with the Russian word *Mir*, which has a different signification in the language of business, the law, and of the educated classes, from what it has in that of the people. In the first case it is identical with the French word *Commune*, being the aggregate of persons living together in the same place, the police jurisdiction of a city, town, or village; but the meaning is quite different in the common conception of the people. Even the literal signification of the word *Mir* indicates the sacredness of the idea, denoting both Commune and World: the Greek *Cosmos* is the only equivalent to the Russian word. I can recollect no German or Romanic proverb in which the power, rights, and sacredness of the Commune are recognized; the Russian language has a great number:—

God alone directs the Mir.
The Mir is great.
The Mir is the surging billow.
The neck and shoulders of the Mir are broad.
Throw everything upon the Mir, it will carry it all.
The tear of the Mir is liquid, but sharp.
The Mir sighs, and the rock is rent asunder.
The Mir sobs, and it re-echoes in the forest.
Trees are felled in the forest, and splinters fly in the Mir.
A thread of the Mir becomes a shirt for the naked.
No one in the world can separate from the Mir.
What belongs to the Mir belongs also to the mother's little son.
What is decided by the Mir must come to pass.
The Mir is unanswerable for the country's defence.

---

1. Reprinted from Baron Von Haxthausen, Robert Farie, trans. *The Russian Empire, Its People, Institutions, and Resources* (London, Chapman and Hall, 1856), v. 2, pp. 228–230.

The patriarchial government, feelings, and organization are in full activity in the life, manners, and customs of the Great Russians. The same unlimited authority which the father exercises over all his children is possessed by the mother over her daughters: the same reverence and obedience are shown to the Communal authorities, the Starostas and While-heads, and to the common father of all, the Czar. The Russian addresses the same word to his real father, to the Starosta, to his proprietor, to the Emperor, and finally to God, viz. Father (*Batiushka*); in like manner he calls every Russian, whether known to him or not, Brother (*Brat*).

✣ *The Necessity of Emancipation: Alexander's Address to the Nobles in Moscow (March 30, 1856)*[1]

You yourselves know that the existing order of ruling over living souls cannot remain unchanged. It is better to abolish serfdom from above than to await the day when it will begin to abolish itself from below.

---

1. Reprinted from Terence Emmons, "The Peasant and Emancipation," in Wayne S. Vucinich, ed. *The Peasant in Nineteenth-Century Russia* (Stanford, Stanford University Press, 1968), pg. 41.

✣ *The Emancipation Manifesto*[1]

Emancipation of the Russian Serfs

St. Petersburg, Sunday

The following is a summary of the Imperial Manifesto proclaiming the emancipation of the serfs, dated the 3d of March (February 19th, O.S.), and published this day:—

---

1. From the London Times, Monday, March 18, 1861.

"The proprietors of landed property preserve the right attached to the same.

"The landed proprietors are, however, to cede to the peasants for their permanent use the dwellings with the ground, which will be allotted to them anew by law, in consideration of the payment of dues.

"During this state of things, which will form a transitory period, the peasants are to be designated 'tributary peasants.'

"The peasants are permitted by law to purchase their dwellings, and, with the consent of the landlords, the land also.

"The peasants will then become free landed proprietors.

"This new order of things is to be carried out throughout the Empire within two years, and until then the peasants remain in their former state of dependence upon the landlords."

✤ *Russian Emancipation Viewed from the Confederate States of America*[1]

Russia, too, has her own troubles. The great measure of emancipation of the serfs keeps that Government anxiously occupied with home policy. It is a wise, bold and generous measure. Above all, it is just and right for the Russian peasants are of as good blood and race as their lords; and nothing is more true than the doctrine contained in our friend, Mr. Spratt's, formula, "Amongst equals equality is right." The serfs of Russia number about thirty-five millions of people—men, women and children;—all this mass of population will be at once raised out of the state of absolute serfdom, and the personal tie which bound them to their lords will be broken. They will still indeed be subject to many restrictions, even as to locomotion; for it would be highly unsafe to set them roving over Russia; but a great beginning will have been made; and that is the way the Czar is consolidating his dynasty.

The St. Petersburg correspondent of the *Nord,* writing on the 25th of February, gives the following account of the emancipation of the Russian serfs: The Council of the Empire held its last sitting to-day on the question of the emancipation of the serfs. The Emperor spoke at considerable length. Other speeches were made, amongst others a remarkable one by Prince Paul Ga-

1. From The Charleston Mercury, Friday, March 29, 1861.

garine. A decision was adoped by a considerable majority, to the following intent:

"Personal liberty is accorded to the serf; all relations between proprietors and peasants cease at once. The latter are to receive as their own property the house they live in and the kitchen garden belonging to it. As regards the allotment (*nadiel*) of the arable land, the Council of the Empire has accepted the settlement of one fourth of the allotment first fixed by the Committee on the Report, according to the different governments, or from one to two *dessiatines* per head."

The Imperial Manifesto is already in the printer's hands, and some 100,000 copies will be issued throughout the different printing offices, under the especial superintendence of the Minister of Justice. The proclamation of the emancipation will, however, not be made on the 3d of March, as announced. It would not be prudent to proclaim "individual liberty,"without, at the same time, explaining the conditions upon which it is granted. At all events, the delay will only be for a few weeks or days, during which time the Carnival will be over, at which period the Russian peasant is not remarkable for exemplary sobriety. It will be, therefore, at the commencement of High Lent that the Imperial Manifesto will be issued. It is, is fact, the most propitious moment for the publication of decree of this importance.

✥ *Russian Emancipation, According to Northern U.S. Newspapers*

The Independent[1]

The plan [of Emancipation] is to give the proprietors time to adjust themselves to the new order of things; to secure to them a fair equivalent for the hitherto compulsory labor of their serfs, and to hold before the serfs the highest motives to industry and good order. Various officers and courts are instituted to see that the scheme of emancipation is fairly administered . . .

What a comment is this humane and Christian act of the Emperor of Russia upon the alleged impossibility of safe and peaceable emancipation! What a comment upon the folly and wickedness of men in this land [i.e., the U.S.], who for the sake of consolidating and perpetuating a worse system of

---

1. From The Independent (New York City), April 11, 1861, p. 4. Special thanks for bringing this and the following passage to our attention go to Professor Richard S. Cramer of the Department of History, San Jose State University and to Douglas Meal, Esq.

slavery than Russia ever knew, are ready to provoke a civil war and to establish for themselves a military despotism! Which of these movements will history recognize as worthy of a Christian nation? Which of them has the sanction of conscience and of the God of justice?

Cincinnati Daily Gazette[1]

The prospective inauguration on the fourth of March, of a President whose alleged fault was a personal dislike to the institution of negro slavery, has been made the occasion of convulsing, perhaps dividing forever, our fondly cherished republic, while all Europe sees in the step that Russia has taken, the first movement toward inward prosperity, freedom and strength. The model, free republic of the nineteenth century [i.e., the U.S.] is to be destroyed on account of abstract questions of respecting the condition of four million blacks, while the hoary despotism of Russia finds safety in the actual emancipation of nearly four times that number of long oppressed whites. Truly, history offers strange contradictions.

---

1. From the Cincinnati Daily Gazette (Cincinnati, Ohio), March 18, 1861, p. 1.

✥ *Alexander on the Need for Further Reform: His Address to the Nobles in 1863*[1]

The reforms prepared, and those already realized, prove my anxiety for the improvement, as far as possible, of the political organization of the country. The past must be a guarantee for the future. The right of initiative in the various parts of the work of gradually perfecting those reforms belongs only to me, and is indissolubly united to the autocratic power confided to me by the Almighty. Those who would frame the laws in future should begin by observing them. I am sure I shall never meet again with such obstacles from my faithful nobles.

---

1. Reprinted from Stephen Graham, *Tsar of Freedom, The Life and Reign of Alexander II* (New Haven, Yale University Press, 1935), pg. 103.

✤ *The Sale of Russian America*[1]

Even as early as during the Oregon Debate in 1846–7, the suggestion had been made that by insisting on the boundary line of 54 degrees 40 minutes, and obtaining a cession from the Emperor Nicholas, the United States might own the whole Pacific coast up to the Arctic Circle. But the slave-holding interest, then dominant in the Federal councils, wanted Southern, not Northern extension. The project was scouted as impracticable, and the line of 54 degrees 40 minutes was given up.

Renewing the subject now through Mr. Stoeckl, the Russian Minister, my father found the Government of the Czar not unwilling to discuss it.

Russia would in no case allow her American possessions to pass into the hands of any European power. But the United States always had been and probably always would be a friend. Russian America was a remote province of the Empire, not easily defensible, and not likely to be soon developed. Under American control it would develop more rapidly and be more easily defended. To Russia, instead of a source of danger, it might become a safeguard. To the United States, it would give a foothold for commercial and naval operations accessible from the Pacific States.

Seward and Gortschakoff were not long in arriving at an agreement upon a subject which, instead of embarrassing with conflicting interests, presented some mutual advantages.

After the graver question of national ownership came the minor one of pecuniary cost. The measure of the value of land to an individual owner is the amount of yearly income it can be made to produce. But national domain gives prestige, power, and safety to the state, and so is not easily to be measured by dollars and cents. Millions cannot purchase these nor compensate for their loss.

However, it was necessary to fix upon a definite sum to be named in the treaty,—not so small as to belittle the transaction in the public eye, not so large as to deprive it of its real character, as an act of friendship on the part of Russia toward the United States. Neither side was especially tenacious about the amount. The previous treaties for the acquisition of territory from France, Spain, and Mexico seemed to afford an index for valuation. The Russians thought, $10,000,000 would be a reasonable amount. Seward proposed $5,000,000. Dividing the difference made it $7,500,000. Then, at Seward's suggestion, the half million was thrown off. But the territory was still subject to some franchises and privileges of the Russian Fur Company. Seward insisted that these should be extinguished by the Russian Government

---

1. Reprinted from Frederick W. Seward, *Reminiscences of War-Time Statesman and Diplomat, 1830–1915* (New York, G. P. Putnam's Sons, 1916), pp. 360–364.

before the transfer, and was willing that $200,000 should be added, on that account, to the $7,000,000.

At this valuation of $7,200,000, the bargain could be deemed satisfactory, even from the standpoint of an individual fisherman, miner, or woodcutter, for the timber, mines, furs, and fisheries would easily yield the annual interest on that sum.

On the evening of Friday, March 29th, Seward was playing whist in his parlour with some of his family, when the Russian Minister was announced.

"I have a dispatch, Mr. Seward, from my government, by cable. The Emperor gives his consent to the cession. Tomorrow, if you like, I will come to the Department, and we can enter upon the treaty."

Seward, with a smile of satisfaction, pushed away the whist-table, saying.

"Why wait till tomorrow, Mr. Stoeckl? Let us make the treaty tonight!"

"But your Department is closed. You have no clerks, and my secretaries are scattered about the town."

"Never mind that," responded Seward. "If you can muster your legation together, before midnight you will find me awaiting you at the Department, which will be open and ready for business."

In less than two hours afterward, light was streaming out of the windows of the Department of State, and apparently business was going on as at midday. By four o'clock on Saturday morning, the treaty was engrossed, signed, sealed, and ready for transmission by the President to the Senate. There was need of this haste, in order to have it acted upon before the end of the session, now near at hand.

On the following morning, while the Senate was considering its favourite theme of administrative delinquencies, the Sergeant at Arms announced, "A message from the President of the United States." Glances were significantly exchanged, with the muttered remark, "Another veto!" Great was the surprise in the chamber, when the Secretary read "A Treaty for the Cession of Russian America." Nor was the surprise lessened, when the Chairman of the Foreign Relations Committee, a leading opponent of the President, rose to move favourable action. His remarks showed easy familiarity with the subject, and that he was prepared to give reasons for the speedy approval of the treaty.

The debate which followed in the Senate was animated and earnest, but in the end the treaty was confirmed without serious opposition. But the purchase was not consummated without a storm of raillery in conversation and ridicule in the press. Russian America was declared to be "a barren, worthless, God-forsaken region," whose only products were "icebergs and polar bears." It was said that the ground was "frozen six feet deep," and "the streams were glaciers." "Walrussia," was suggested as a name for it, if it deserved to have any. Vegetation was said to be "limited to mosses"; and "no useful animals could live there." There might be some few "wretched fish," only fit for "wretched Esquimaux" to eat. But nothing could be raised or dug there. Seven millions of good money were going to be wasted in buying it. Many millions more would have to be spent in holding and defending it,—for it was "remote, inhospitable, and inaccessible." It was "Seward's Folly." It was "Johnson's Polar Bear Garden." It was "an egregious blunder," "a bad bargain," palmed off on "a silly Administration" by the "shrewd Russians," etc.

Most of these jeers and flings were from those who disliked the President and blamed Seward for remaining in his Cabinet. Perhaps unwillingness to admit that anything wise or right could be done by "Andy Johnson's Administration" was the real reason for the wrath visited upon the unoffending territory. The feeling of hostility to the purchase was so strong that the House of Representatives would not take action toward accepting the territory or appropriate any money to pay for it.

The Russian Government courteously waived any demand for immediate payment and signified readiness to make the final transfer whenever the United States might desire. Accordingly commissioners were appointed, who proceeded to Sitka.

On a bright day in August, 1867, with brief but impressive ceremonies, amid salutes from the Russian and American naval vessels, the American flag was raised over the new territory to be thenceforth known as "Alaska."

✜ *The Future of Russia, From Herzen's Memoirs*[1]

Thirty years ago, the Russia of the *future* existed exclusively among a few boys, hardly more than children, so small and inconspicuous that there was room for them under the heels of the jackboots of the autocracy—yet in them lay the heritage of December 14, the heritage of a purely national Russia, as well as of the learning of all humanity. This new life struggled on like the grass sprouting at the mouth of the still smouldering crater.

In the very maw of the monster these children, so unlike other children, grew, developed and began to live a different life. Weak, insignificant, unsupported, and persecuted by everybody, they might have easily perished, leaving no trace, but they *survived,* or, if they died on their way, all did not die with them. They were the rudimentary cells, the embryos of history, barely perceptible and barely existing—like all embryos.

Little by little, groups of them were formed.

---

1. Reprinted from Thomas Riha, *Readings in Russian Civilization* (Chicago, the University of Chicago Press, 1969), v. 2, pp. 324–325.

The leading characteristic of them all was a profound feeling of aversion for official Russia, for their environment, and at the same time the urge to escape out of it—and, in some of them, a vehement desire to change the contemporary state of affairs.

✤ Ivan Aksakov on the Assassination of Alexander II[1]

The Emperor is murdered; the same Emperor who was the greatest benefactor to his country, who emancipated tens of millions of Russian peasants, bestowing upon them human and civil rights. He is murdered; not for personal vengeance, not for booty, but precisely because he is the Emperor, the crowned head, the representative, the first man of his country, that vital, single man who personified the very essence, the whole image, the whole strength and power, of Russia. From time immemorial that power has constituted the strength of the country. The attempt directed against the person of the Tsar is always directed against the whole people; but in this case the whole historical principle of the national life has been attacked, the autocratic power bestowed upon the Emperor by the country itself . . .

But that injustice is exactly what we do not possess. Thanks to God, and thanks to that martyr-Emperor so brutally murdered, our fourth class, our peasantry, comprising almost 80 per cent of the whole realm, now possesses land, organization, and the most complete self-government. To this very day, that fourth class is the keeper of our historical instinct, of our religion, and of the whole element of our political organism. They, and not the so-called Intelligentsia, are the real supporters of our country . . . .

---

1. Reprinted from Hans Kohn, ed. *The Mind of Modern Russia* (New Brunswick, Rutgers University Press, 1955), pp. 112–114.

✤ A French Diplomat's Remarks at the Funeral of Alexander II[1]

"Have a good look at this martyr. He was a great tsar and deserved a kinder fate . . .

Think of all the resistance he had to overcome to abolish serfdom and restore the foundation of rural economy. Think that thirty million men owe their affranchisement to him. . . . And his administrative reforms! He aimed at nothing less than the destruction of the arbitrary bureaucracy and social privilege. In the judicial sphere he established equality before the law, assured the independence of the magistrates, abolished corporal punishment, instituted the jury. And this was done by the immediate successor of the despot Nicholas I! . . .

Finally, on the morning of his death, he was working on a reform which would have surpassed all the others, would have launched Russia irrevocably along the track of the modern world: the granting of a parliamentary charter . . . And the Nihilists have killed him! . . . But mark the odd coincidence of history, the strange irony of things. Lincoln, the emancipator of the American negroes, was also assassinated. Now, it was the deliverance of the negroes which brought in its train, on the other side of the world, the affranchisement of the *moujiks*. Alexander did not intend that Russia should remain the only serf-holding nation in the Christian world. . . . Oh, a liberator's is a dangerous job!"

---

1. Reprinted from W. E. Mosse, *Alexander II and the Modernization of Russia* (London, The English Universities, LTD, 1966), pp. 180–181.

Chapter Eight

ALEXANDER III AND THE RISE OF RUSSIAN RADICALISM

Alexander III succeeded his father in 1881 and, although he initially wished to fulfill his father's plan to convene the consultative assembly was pursuaded from acting on any reform by Konstantin Pobedonostsev, the reactionary Procurator of the Holy Synod (who was the emperor's chief tutor and closest advisor). Pobedonostsev closely monitered the press and the curriculum at the universities. He also ensured that reactionaries were appointed to key posts in Alexander III's government. Members of the People's Will and revolutionaries of all sorts were executed or exiled to Siberia.

During Alexander III's reign (1881–94), however, revolutionary activity increased as rural and industrial working conditions deteriorated. In a period of forty years after the Emancipation Manifesto was issued, land values and rentals increased while the amount of land per male decreased fifty percent as a result of population growth. The increasing importation of American grain into Western Europe in this period lowered the price of Russian wheat and barley, further exacerbating the problems of Russian agriculture. Certain critics would emerge, such as the Socialist Revolutionaries (1898–1901) led by Victor Chernov, which advocated radical land redistribution as a remedy for growing land hunger.

Among the groups which emerged in this period of revolutionary activity was the first Russian Marxist party, the Emancipation of Labor (founded by 1883). Officially banned, the party worked underground to organize and educate the industrial laborers. Some early leaders, such as George Plekhanov, who has been called "the father of Russian Marxism," were brought into the movement from agrarian reform groups. According to Marxist theory, urban industrial workers (the proletariat*) must form into a revolutionary body in order for the socialist revolution to occur. The census of 1897, however, reveals that industrial workers in the empire numbered only fourteen million, compared to the one hundred million peasants in rural Russia. Karl Marx wrote, however, in the preface to a Russian translation of* Das Kapital *that a genuine socialist revolution could occur in Russia if the agricultural workers were mobilized.*

*Among the radicals who believed that this could occur was Vladimir Ily-
ich Ulyanov, who took the name Lenin. Lenin was involved in Russian Marxist circles from 1893, and in 1903 his unique interpretation of Marxism, in
which a revolutionary elite was to be utilized, became the majority position
among Russian Marxists, then known by the name of the Social Democratic
Party. These Social Democrats who followed Lenin came to be called Bol-
sheviks (as opposed to the non-Leninist Marxists, called Mensheviks, who
were led by Martov).*

*Count Serge Witte served in several capacities within the governments of
Alexander III and Nicholas II. While he was Minister of Finance from 1892
to 1903, he encouraged economic growth by expanding the railroad system
(especially across Siberia), acquiring foreign loans to finance industrial projects, and raising tariffs to protect Russian products. The first, second and
sixth passages are from Witte's memoirs, and describe the character and
habits of Alexander III, the construction of the Trans-Siberian Railroad, and
the death of the Emperor (translated by Abraham Yarmolinsky).*

*Industrial working conditions became more wretched as the scale and the
pace of the process of industrialization increased in Russia. Consequently,
labor unrest become evident in number of cities within the empire around
the turn of the century. Our third selection was written by P. Timofeev, who
has been described as a member of an emerging "worker-intelligentsia."
The passage concerns the problems encountered in searching for work in
industry (translated by Victoria E. Bonnell). The fourth passage is taken
from Marx's Preface to the 1882 Russian edition of the* Manifesto of the
Communist Party *(edited by Robert C. Tucker). The fifth passage was written by Lenin in his tract entitled "What is to be Done?" and explains the
need for Bolshevik activism.*

The Character and Habits of Alexander III, According to Serge Witte[1]

Alexander III was undeniably a man of limited education. I cannot agree, however, with those who would class him as unintelligent. Though lacking perhaps in mental keenness, he was undoubtedly gifted with the broad sympathetic understanding which in a ruler is often far more important than rational brilliancy.

Neither in the Imperial family nor among the nobility was there anyone who better appreciated the value of a ruble or a kopeck than Emperor Alexander III. He made an ideal treasurer for the Russian people, and his economical temperament was of incalculable assistance in the solution of Russia's financial problems. Had not the Emperor doggedly warded off the incessant raids upon the Russian treasury and checked the ever-present impulse to squander the public funds accumulated by the sweat and blood of the people, Vyshnegradski and myself could never have succeeded in putting the nation back upon its feet financially.

Alexander III's prudence in government expenditures was matched by his personal thrift. Abhorring luxury and lavish spending, he led an extremely simple life. When he grew tired of his own table, he would ask for a common soldier's or a hunter's meal. This economy was sometimes carried too far. The Imperial table was always relatively poor, and the food served at the Court Marshal's board was sometimes such as to endanger the health. Alexander III was extremely economical with his wearing apparel. I had a curious proof of this when I accompanied the Emperor on one of his railway trips. Since I found it impossible, on account of my responsibility, to sleep of nights, I would often catch glimpses of His Majesty's valet mending the Emperor's trousers. On one occasion I asked him why he didn't give his master a new pair instead of mending the old so often. "Well, I would rather have it that way," he answered, "but His Majesty won't let me. He insists on wearing his garments until they are threadbare. It is the same with his boots. Not only does he wear them as long as possible, but he refuses to put on expensive ones. If I should bring him patent leather boots, he would angrily thrown them out of the window." The Emperor's dislike of the expensive included gorgeous rooms. For this reason he never stayed in the

---

1. From *The Memoirs of Count Witte* by Count Serge Witte. Copyright 1920, 1921 by Doubleday, a division of Bantam, Doubleday, Dell Publishing Group, Inc. Used by permission of Doubleday, a division of Bantam Doubleday Dell Publishing Group, Inc. pp. 38–41.

Photo: St. Isaac's Cathedral in St. Petersburg.

Winter Palace, but always occupied the unpretentious quarters of Anichkov or Gatchina. There he took small rooms and lived frugally. He tolerated the Court's luxury as an unavoidable formality, but he always longed for a different mode of existence and created it for himself in his private life.

✜ *The Construction of the Trans-Siberian Railroad*[1]

The construction of railroads fell entirely within the authority of my Ministry. In those years the Russian railroad system was in a process of continuous and rapid growth. Naturally, the numerous concession seekers kept flocking to my reception room. Among them there were a great many members of our highest aristocracy. It was then that I found out of what inferior stuff all these people with ancient names were made. Unlimited greed seemed to be their chief characteristic. These men who at Court functions wore princely airs were ready to crawl on all fours in my office, provided they could thus obtain some financial advantage. For many years some of these scoundrels and hypocrites have been holding the highest Court positions and, at least outwardly, they have been intimate with the Imperial family.

Speaking of railroad building it must be borne in mind that those years the Government was pursuing a consistent policy of railroad construction and operation by the State. This policy involved a series of transactions designed to redeem the privately owned roads and turn them over to the State.

It will not be an exaggeration to say that the vast enterprise of constructing the great Siberian Railway was carried out owing to my efforts, supported, of course by Emperor Alexander III, and then by Emperor Nicholas II. The idea of connecting European Russia with Vladivostok by rail was one of the most cherished dreams of Alexander III. He spoke to me about it in the course of one of my first conferences with him following my appointment as Minister of Ways of Communication. As is known, Czarevitch Nicholas, the present Emperor, during his trip through the Far East, inaugurated, on May 19, 1891, the construction of the Ussurian Railroad, connecting Vladivostok with Khabarovsk. The Emperor complained that in spite of his efforts, which extended over ten years, his dream had failed to materialize owing to the opposition of the Committee of Ministers and the Imperial

1. From *The Memoirs of Count Witte* by Count Serge Witte. Copyright 1920, 1921 by Doubleday, a division of Bantam, Doubleday, Dell Publishing Group, Inc. Used by permission of Doubleday, a division of Bantam Doubleday Dell Publishing Group, Inc. pp. 52–53.

Council. He took my promise that I would bend my energies to the accomplishment of his desire.

In my capacity of Minister of Ways of Communication and later as Minister of Finances, both during the reign of Alexander III and afterwards, I persistently advocated the idea of the necessity of constructing the great Siberian Railway. As much as the former Ministers thwarted the plan, so I, remembering my promise to the Emperor, sought to advance it. As Minister of Finances, I was in a peculiarly favorable position with regard to furthering the project, for what was most needed for the construction of the railway was money. Had I remained Minister of Ways of Communication, I would have had to face the opposition of the Minister of Finances.

I devoted myself body and soul to the task, yet Emperor Alexander III did not live to see the realization of his dream, and it was only under Nicholas II that the immense railroad was completed. I was aided by the circumstance that the young Emperor took a personal interest in the matter. At my instance, while his father was still alive, he was appointed head of the Siberian Railroad Committee, which I had formed to promote the construction of the railroad. This committee was empowered to eliminate all manner of unnecessary delay and had the authority over both the administrative and the legislative matters involved in the construction.

✧ *Looking for Work in Russian Industry*[1]

I shall now try and describe the ordeals which the worker has to go through to get a job. How does a worker find work in a factory?

Here in Russia, everything is done by means of "family" connections. Let us suppose you are a metalworker, and you have arrived in a totally strange town. The first thing you have to do is find a factory. In order to do that, you walk several miles to the outskirts of the town. You can always tell when you are getting close to a factory because of the buildings: the dirty taverns and the even dirtier shops and beer halls. A little further on you notice smoke rising from the factory chimneys; then you see the chimneys and finally the factory building itself.

Along one of these walls you will find the factory gates and next to them a small building called the "entry office" where you have to go. If it is early morning or around lunchtime, you will probably find several people

---

1. Reprinted from Victoria E. Bonnell, ed. *The Russian Worker: Life and Labor Under the Tsarist Regime* (Berkeley, University of California Press, 1983), pp. 84–85.

dressed like yourself waiting there. They are also looking for a job and probably waiting to find a foreman or friend who can give them a reference. You go up to them and start a conversation.

"Hi, pal. You got a light?" Then you go on to ask where he worked before, what his trade is, and so on, and finally you ask the question: "Do they need any metalfitters here?"

✛ Marx: Russia and Revolution[1]

The Communist Manifesto had as its object the proclamation of the inevitably impending dissolution of modern bourgeois property. But in Russia we find, face to face with the rapidly developing capitalist swindle and bourgeois landed property, just beginning to develop, more than half the land owned in common by the peasants. Now the question is: Can the Russian *obshchina*, though greatly undermined, yet a form of the primeval common ownership of land, pass directly to the higher form of communist common? Or, on the contrary, must it first pass through the same process of dissolution as constitutes the historical evolution of the West?

The only answer to that possible today is this: If the Russian Revolution becomes the signal for the proletarian revolution in the West, so that both complement each other, the present Russian common ownership of land may serve as the starting-point for a communist development.

London, January 21, 1882   *Karl Marx   Friedrich Engels*

---

1. Taken from the Preface the 1882 Russian edition of the *Manifesto of the Communist Party,* in Robert C. Tucker, ed. *The Marx-Engels Reader,* second edition, (New York, W.W. Norton and Company, 1978) pp. 471–472.

✛ Lenin on the Need for Activism[1]

The spontaneous rise of the masses in Russia proceeded (and continues) with such rapidity that the young untrained social democrats proved unfitted for

---

1. Reprinted from Helmut Gruber, *International Communism in the Era of Lenin* (Garden City, N.Y., Anchor Books/Doubleday and Company, 1972) pp. 18–19.

the gigantic tasks that confronted them. This lack of training is our common misfortune, the misfortune of *all* Russian social democrats. The rise of the masses proceeded and spread uninterruptedly and continuously; it not only continued in the places it commenced in, but it spread to new localities and to new strata of the population (influenced by the labor movement, the ferment among the students and the intellectuals generally, and even among the peasantry revived). Revolutionaries, however, *lagged behind* this rise of the masses in both their "theories" and in their practical activity; they failed to establish an uninterrupted organization having continuity with the past, and capable of *leading* the whole movement. . . .

We said that a social democrat, if he really believes it is necessary to develop the political consciousness of the proletariat, must "go among all classes of the people." This gives rise to the questions: How is this to be done? Have we enough forces to do this? Is there a base for such work among all the other classes? Will this not mean a retreat, or lead to a retreat from the class point-of-view?

We must "go among all classes of the people" as theoreticians, as propagandists, as agitators, and as organizers.

✤ *The Death of Alexander III*[1]

On October 19 (31), as the result of an alarming report from Yalta regarding His Majesty's critical condition, a special prayer was ordered at the Kazan Cathedral. Members of all classes of the population, including the students, thronged the church and prayed fervently for the Czar's life. The next day the people received the sad news that the Emperor had passed away. He died with beautiful equanimity, mindful only of the welfare of the dear ones left behind.

The Emperor's body was taken from Yalta to St. Petersburg. On the way it lay in state for a day at the Uspensky Cathedral in Moscow, whose inhabitants flocked to do final homage to their revered ruler. When the body reached the northern capital, there was a solemn procession from the station to the Cathedral of St. Peter and Paul. The ceremonies were highly impressive, yet marked at every point with the noble simplicity which had characterized Alexander III's reign. Several times, once throughout the night, I was among those who stood guard over the Emperor's body at the Cathedral and I saw the people come in masses to pay the last honours to their beloved monarch.

1. From *The Memoirs of Count Witte* by Count Serge Witte. Copyright 1920, 1921 by Doubleday, a division of Bantam, Doubleday, Dell Publishing Group, Inc. Used by permission of Doubleday, a division of Bantam Doubleday Dell Publishing Group, Inc. pp. 46–47.

Chapter Nine

NICHOLAS II AND THE TWILIGHT OF IMPERIAL RUSSIA

Nicholas II succeeded his father in 1894. His reign (1894–1917) was plagued by internal and external difficulties. In the agricultural sector, famines occurred in 1895–96 and 1901, and land rents doubled in this period. Massive unemployment affected Russian industry, as well. Despite Minister of Finance Witte's plans the empire faced a severe economic crisis in the first few years after the turn of the century. Several members of Nicholas's government (including Count Plehve) believed that the only way the monarchy could salvage its prestige was by victory in a war. Increasing tensions with Japan over possession of Manchuria led to the Japanese attack on the Russian Pacific coast base of Port Arthur (Feb 5, 1904). Many governmental officials welcomed the war as a means of distracting the people from the economic hardships afflicting the empire.

Conflicting claims for suzerainty over Manchuria stretched back several decades, but Japan had assumed a dominant position in East Asia following its defeat of China in an 1894–95 war fought over control of Korea. During the suppression of the Boxer Rebellion in 1900, however, Russian troops occupied Manchuria and would not leave despite repeated American and British-backed Japanese appeals (1901–04). Fearful of losing its preeminent position in East Asia, the pro-expansionist Japanese regime attacked Port Arthur.

The imperial Russian army, despite its size, was soundly defeated on land by better-equipped Japanese forces, and the imperial navy was decisively defeated by the Japanese in the Battle of Tsushima Straits. The Treaty of Portsmouth (Sept. 1905), which was mediated by American President Theodore Roosevelt, ended the war. Although the regime lost only its leases in southern Manchuria and Sakhalin Island, according to the rather generous provisions of the treaty, many of Nicholas' subjects criticized his government for the heavy casualties and wasted resources spent in a humiliating defeat. The domestic economy had continued to deteriorate during the war, and unrest broke out in many cities of the empire after news spread of the territorial concessions (however minimal they actually were) at Portsmouth. This general unrest soon developed into a full-scale revolution whose aim was to topple the tsarist regime.

Reacting to defeats incurred in the war, the Union of Liberation, a group comprised of liberals, urban professionals, and zemstvo *officials, had agitated for change in 1904. The Social Democrats and Social Revolutionaries also soon demanded change as a result of the war. While radical demands were being made by various groups, Count Plehve was assassinated. Police-controlled trade unions were then organized by an agent of the Moscow security police, Colonel Zubatov, in order to give dissatisfied workers a means by which they could air their grievances, but which would allow the government to screen out committed revolutionaries. A former prison chaplain, Fr. George Gapon, headed a Zubatov-controlled union which called for higher wages and a reduction of hours in the work day (down to ten hours a day). Radicals, however, managed to infiltrate the union and made political demands in addition to the economic ones: land for peasants, the creation of a parliament, and the toleration of free speech. Gapon led two hundred thousand St. Petersburg workers in a peaceful protest march to the Winter Palace on January 9, 1905. The day is remembered as "Bloody Sunday" because the palace guard, fearing violence, fired on the crowd and killed hundreds (perhaps as many as a thousand) marchers. Ironically, Nicholas was not even at the Winter Palace at the time. Nicholas' uncle, Grand Duke Sergei (who was governor-general of Moscow) was assassinated in February, and the regime then declared its intention to create a legislative assembly. By the summer, however, no real steps were as yet taken by Nicholas towards this goal, and a "Union of Unions" was created by Paul Miliukov and his followers from the* zemstvos *to agitate for the creation of a constituent assembly. Nicholas then agreed in August to create an Imperial Duma.*

When in the fall progress towards reform was still not made by the government, a railroad workers strike occurred in St. Petersburg on October 8. This was followed by a general strike in the cities and on the rail lines. With the national economy at a virtual standstill, Nicholas was compelled to issue the October 30 Manifesto, granting full civil rights and the creation of a Duma which possessed full legislative powers. The government assisted the peasants in their redemption payments and by providing loans for the purchase of land through a peasant land bank. The press was given greater freedom and a partial political amnesty was proclaimed. An Octobrist Party was formed by the moderates who were supportive of the reforms, but some radicals formed a Soviet of Workers' Deputies in an attempt to continue the strike and topple the government.

Two more attempts to call for a resumption of the general strike failed, and the government, realizing that the radicals no longer had much support, arrested the leaders of the Soviet on December 3.

Four Dumas were convened, however, over the next eleven years. The first was dissolved only two and a half months after its inception because it quarrelled with Peter Stolypin (Minister of the Interior, then Prime Minister) over the issue of land reform. Stolypin envisioned a plan whereby individual peasants could leave the mir *and cultivate private farms, especially in some* of the less-populated regions of the empire. He was moderately successful, and a new group of landowning peasants were thus supportive of the reforms and loyal to the tsarist regime.

The Second Duma (1907) was marred by the fact that many of the moderate Constitutional Democrats (Kadets) failed to participate, leaving leftist and rightist radicals who could cooperate neither with each other nor with the government. Stolypin dissolved it after just four months and arrested sixteen Social Democrats for allegedly plotting to overthrow the government. The conservatives and Octobrists who formed the majority within the Third Duma (1907–11), however, managed to cooperate with the government and pass some military and educational reforms. Stolypin was assassinated, however, in September 1911, by a Social Revolutionary (six months after dissolving the Duma). The Fourth Duma (1912-17) did little more than criticize the regime.

In the conservative climate that characterized the last years of Nicholas' reign, the Union of True Russian People was formed, which conducted rightwing terrorist operations against leftists through paramilitary bands called Black Hundreds. The Black Hundreds ultimately received official government recognition.

Nicholas' government justified Russian involvement in the First World War (to be discussed more fully in Volume Three) as an attempt to galvanize the support of the loyal subjects of the tsar in assisting fellow Slavs in the Balkans (the Serbs) against the imperialistic encroachments of the Austrians (reminiscent of Russian involvement in the Greek and Serbian struggles for independence against the Turks under Nicholas I). Unfortunately for the tsarist regime, the German army of the Hohenzollerns proved to be too great an adversary and the poorly-equipped Russian forces were repeatedly beaten on the Eastern Front. To further demoralize the country, the "Rasputin Scandal" occurred, in which key governmental figures were dismissed by the tsarina Alexandra at the behest of the so-called "Mad Monk," Gregory Rasputin (while Nicholas was away at the front). The immediate causes of the February/March Revolution in 1917 which brought the Provisional Government to power were the costly failure of the Brusilov Offensive (into Galicia, 1916) and the dismissal of the Duma. Nicholas recognized that he was no longer in command of either the army or the government, and he abdicated on March 2, 1917. When his brother, the Grand Duke Michael, refused the throne on March 3, the Old Order in Russia ended (more in Volume Three).

The first passage in this section is taken from the memoirs of Count Sergei Witte, who served the government of Nicholas II in several capacities (most notably as Minister of Finance), translated by Abraham Yarmolinsky. The passage consists of Witte's thoughts of Nicholas the man, and can be compared to Witte's remarks concerning Nicholas' father, Alexander III, which appear in the previous chapter. Constantine Pobedonostsev served as the Procurator of the Holy Synod from 1880 to 1905, and was the official *tutor to Alexander III and Nicholas II, in addition to serving on the State Council. Our second passage consists an excerpt from Pobedonostsev's* Reflections of a Russian Statesman *concerning his view of the proper role of the press (translated by Robert Crozier Long). Our third selection is on Nicholas II and Japan, taken from Witte's memoirs. Baron Nicholas Wrangel wrote an interesting memoir covering the years 1847–1920, which he subtitled "From Serfdom to Bolshevism." We have taken our fourth passage, concerning the Russo-Japanese War, from this work. Significantly, he mentions the early military career of his son, Peter Nikolaievich, who would go on to become the commander of the counter-revolutionary White forces in the Russian Civil War (translated by Brian and Beatrix Lunn). From Witte's memoir we have taken our fifth passage, on the government Vodka monopoly during the Russo-Japanese War. The sixth text is on Bloody Sunday, taken from the memoir of Baron Wrangel. The seventh, eighth, and ninth passages come from Witte's memoir: the 1905 Revolution, the "loan that saved Russia," and Stolypin's land reform. Our tenth passage is an excerpt from a speech made by Stolypin to the Duma (dated May 10, 1907), preserved by his daughter, Maria Petrovna Von Bock, on population growth in the late imperial period (translated by Margaret Patoski).*

Gregory Efimovich Rasputin is one of the most controversial figures in Russian history. He began his career as a wandering mystic in Siberia, and became a successful starets, *or popular man of God, in Kazan and St. Petersburg. Through his relationship with Anna Vyrubova, a friend of Empress Alexandra, he came to exert a tremendous influence over the royal family, and ultimately had an influence on the highest levels of government. Particularly important in his rise were his supposed powers of hypnotism and his alleged ability to assist in the cessation of the hemophiliac bleeding of the heir Alexei. The tremendous influence he exerted on the government was seen as harmful by many courtiers. Our next passage comes from Prince Felix Yusupov, who participated in Rasputin's murder on December 17, 1916. According to Yusupov, those who participated in the murder "believed that Russia was saved, and that with Rasputin's disappearance a new era had dawned."*

Our twelfth passage is an excerpt from the secret telegram sent by Izvolsky, the Russian Ambassador to France, to the Russian Foreign Secretary, Sazanov, regarding the position of Germany and Austria on the eve of the First World War. The thirteenth passage is taken from Nicholas' remarks made to the Duma members and members of the State Council on August 8, 1914, after the outbreak of the First World War.

Our fourteenth passage is an excerpt from a police report from Petrograd (St. Petersburg, which name was changed in the course of the First World War) dated October 14– November 14, 1916 (translated by R. J. Minney). The report demonstrates how desperate the domestic economic and social situation had become as a consequence of the war. Our final passage is a description of soldiers who had gone over to the side of anti-tsarist revolutionaries in 1916, reported by Baron Wrangel.

✤ *The Coronation of Nicholas II*[1]

The coronation of Emperor Nicholas II, which took place on May 14 (Russian style), 1896, was marked by a sad and ominous occurrence; nearly two thousand people perished on the Khodynka Field, in Moscow, where refreshments and amusements had been prepared for the populace. A few hours after the Khodynka disaster their Majesties attended a concert conducted by the celebrated Safonov. I vividly recollect a brief conversation which I had at that concert with the Chinese plenipotentiary Li Hung Chang, who was at that time in St. Petersburg on official business. He was curious to know the details of the catastrophe and I told him that nearly two thousand people must have perished.

"But His Majesty," he said, "does not know it, does he?"

"Of course, he knows," I replied. "All the facts of the matter must have already been reported to him."

"Well," remarked the Chinaman, "I don't see the wisdom of that. I remember when I was Governor-General, ten million people died from the bubonic plague in the provinces confined to my charge, yet our Emperor knew nothing about it. Why disturb him uselessly?"

I thought to myself that, after all, we were ahead of the Chinese.

A gorgeous evening party was scheduled for the same day, to be given by the French Ambassador, Marquis de Montebello. We expected that the party would be called off, because of the Khodynka disaster. Nevertheless, it took place, as if nothing had happened, and the ball was opened by their Majesties dancing a quadrille.

The Emperor's character may be said to be essentially feminine. Someone has observed that Nature granted him masculine attributes by mistake. At first any official coming in personal contact with him would stand high in his eyes. His Majesty would even go beyond the limits of moderation in showering favours upon his servant, especially if the latter had been appointed by him personally and not by his father. Before long, however, His Majesty would become indifferent to his favourite and, in the end, develop an animus against him. The ill-feeling apparently came from the consciousness that the person in question had been an unworthy object of his, Nicholas's, favours. I may observe here that His Majesty does not tolerate about his person anybody he considers more intelligent than himself or anybody with opinions differing from those of the court camarilla.

---

1. From *The Memoirs of Count Witte* by Count Serge Witte. Copyright 1920, 1921 by Doubleday, a division of Bantam, Doubleday, Dell Publishing Group, Inc. Used by permission of Doubleday, a division of Bantam Doubleday Dell Publishing Group, Inc. pp. 181–183.

Photo: Facade of the Winter Palace in St. Petersburg.

✤ *Pobedonostsev on the Press*[1]

There is nothing more remarkable in this century of advancement than the development of journalism to its present state as a terribly active social force. The importance of the Press first began to increase after the Revolution of July 1830, it doubled its influence after the Revolution of 1848; since then it has grown in power not only year by year but day by day. Already Governments have begun to measure their strength against this new force, and it has become impossible to imagine not only public but even individual life without the newspaper; so that the suppression of newspapers, if it were possible, would mean as much to daily life as the cessation of railway communications. Without doubt, the newspaper serves the world as a powerful instrument of culture. But while we acknowledge the convenience and profit derived from the dissemination of knowledge among the people, and from the interchange of thought and opinion, we cannot ignore the dangers imminent from the unbounded growth of the Press; we cannot refuse to recognise with a feeling of terror, the fatal, mysterious, and disintegrating force which threatens the future of humanity.

Every day the newspaper brings us a mass of varied news. How much of this is of real use to our lives, and to our educational development? How much is fit to feed in our souls the sacred flame of aspiration unto good? How much is there not to flatter our baser instincts and impulses? We are told that the newspaper gives what the taste of readers demands, that its level reaches the level of the reader's taste. But to this we may reply that the demand would not be so great were the supply less energetically pushed.

If news alone were published the case would be different; but no, it is offered in a special form, embellished with personal opinions, and accompanied by anonymous but very decided commentaries. Papers controlled by serious persons of course exist, but such are few, while to the making of newspapers there is no end; and no morning passes without some writer, unknown to me, whom, perhaps, I should not care to know, obtruding upon me his views, expressed with all the authority of public opinion. What is graver still, however, is that this newspaper addresses not only a single class, but all men, some of whom can barely spell out a page of print, and offers to each a ready-made judgment upon everything, in such a seductive form that, little by little, by force of habit, the reader loses all wish for, and feels absolved from the duty of, forming his own opinions. Some have no ability for forming opinions, and accept mechanically the opinions of their newspapers; while others, born with a capacity for original thought, in the trials and anxieties of daily life have not the time to think, and welcome the newspaper which does their thinking for them. The

---

1. Reprinted from Konstantin P. Pobedonostsev, Robert Crozier Long, trans. *Reflections of a Russian Statesman* (London, 1898), pp. 69–71, 73.

harm that results from this is too visible, especially in our time when powerful currents of thought are everywhere in action, wearing down the corners and distinctions of individual thought, reducing to uniformity the so-called public opinion, and weakening all independent development of thought, of will, and of character. Moreover, for many of the people the newspaper is the only source of education—a contemptible, pretended education—the varied mass of news and information found in the newspaper being taken by its readers as real knowledge, with which he proceeds to arm himself complacently. This we may take as one of the reasons why our age brings forth so few *complete* individuals, so few men of character. The modern Press is like the fabled hero who, having inscribed upon his visor some mysterious characters, the symbols of divine truth, struck all his enemies with terror, till one intrepid warrior rubbed from his helm the mysterious letters. On the visor of our Press to-day is written the legend "Public Opinion," and its influence is irresistible.

If the journalist is to attract attention, he must raise his voice to a scream. This his trade requires, and exaggeration capable of passing into pathos becomes for him his second nature. When he enters upon a controversy he is ready to denounce his adversary as a fool, a rascal, or a dunce, to heap upon him unimaginable insults—this costs his conscience nothing; it is required by journalistic etiquette. His cries resemble the protestations of a trader in the market-place when he cheats his customers.

✤ *Nicholas II and Japan*[1]

At heart, His Majesty was for an aggressive policy, but as usual his mind was a house divided against itself. He kept on changing his policy from day to day. He tried to deceive both the Viceroy of the Far East and the Commander-in-Chief of the army, but, of course, most of the time he deceived nobody but himself.

He became involved in the Far Eastern adventure because of his youth, his natural animosity against Japan, where an attempt had been made on his life (he never speaks of that occurrence), and, finally, because of a hidden craving for a victorious war. I am even inclined to believe that, had there been no clash with Japan, war would have flared up on the Indian frontier, or, most probably, in Turkey, with the Bosphorus as the apple of discord. From there it would have spread to other regions.

---

1. From *The Memoirs of Count Witte* by Count Serge Witte. Copyright 1920, 1921 by Doubleday, a division of Bantam, Doubleday, Dell Publishing Group, Inc. Used by permission of Doubleday, a division of Bantam Doubleday Dell Publishing Group, Inc. p. 186.

✢ *The Russo-Japanese War*[1]

On the 26th January, 1904, Japan attacked the Russian fleet without warning and sunk three of our ships. Next day war was declared.

I do not believe that a war has ever been less popular. The Russian people had never heard of Japan, and there was therefore no reason for any additional hostility, as there was in the case of Turkey, Poland, or England. Those who were in a position to judge, those, in fact, who were more or less civilised, realised that the results of the conflict, whatever they might be, were bound to be harmful to Russia.

If Russia were victorious, the Czar, by which I mean his Government (for the Czar himself was known to be only a shadow), would make use of the opportunity to strengthen absolutism and to treat Russia more than ever before as a conquered country. If, on the other hand, the campaign were lost, revolution would result and, as any man of common sense knew, revolution in Russia would not be a revolution in the European sense of the word—that is, a mere change in the form of government—but would result in massacres, in rivers of blood and in the complete ruin of every vestige of civilisation, as indeed happened a few years later.

The war was disastrous from the very start. In March the Japanese sank the ship carrying the Admiral commanding the Russian squadron; in April there was the defeat at Turentchen and the Japanese attack at Eidsyvo; in August there was the heavy defeat at Liayan, which, as we learned after the war from the Japanese themselves, would have been a decisive victory for the Russians if Kuropatkin had not turned tail at the last moment. Then, finally, there was the disastrous retreat to Mukden.

But at St. Petersburg people were still saying that everything was all right. A new fleet was to sail for the Far East, Port Arthur was still holding out, and when the fleet arrived a very little fighting would settle the matter.

There were rejoicings in high quarters. The trivial disappointment in Manchuria was a small account compared with the auspicious event which had just taken place. On the 30th of July an heir to the throne had been born. The future of the throne was assured and therefore that of Russia also.

Port Arthur capitulated on the 22nd December.

We were uneasy at home. We had had fairly frequent news of our son at the beginning of the war. We heard that he had been decorated. Then we read a distressing account in a paper of a man who got sunstroke during the fighting. The correspondent had seen with his own eyes the Cossack lieuten-

1. Reprinted from Brian and Beatrix Lunn, co-trans. *The Memoirs of Baron N. Wrangel, 1847–1920*, pp. 205–210. Copyright 1927 by J. B. Lippincott Company, reprinted by permission of HarperCollins.

ant, Baron Wrangel, former officer in the Horse Guards, being carried away dead on a stretcher. Later we had a telegram from him himself, reading: "Health good, have just been promoted full lieutenant for services rendered on the battle-field." And then for some months we heard nothing.

At last he suddenly turned up one day. He had already reached the rank of captain, but his condition was deplorable. He had been invalided home to recuperate.

He was hardly out of bed before he started pulling every wire he could to be passed fit to rejoin his regiment. Fortunately they laughed at him and told him to go and look at himself in the glass and go back to bed.

My friend Doshturov told me that he had been told at the War Office that my son was considered to be an officer with a brilliant future before him. Doshturov was delighted, as he had said so too.

What our son told us was not particularly reassuring. He said that the army in the field, both men and regimental officers were admirable, that the men were well-disciplined, would endure any hardships and were steady under fire, but they were short of many things, and the Staff were for the most part deplorable. Those who had capability were generally turned on to jobs for which they were unfit. For instance, General Mistshenko, an unrivalled artillery expert, had been placed in command of a cavalry corps of the advance guard, although he had never been on a horse, while General Rennenkampf, a cavalry general if ever there was one, had been given the command of an infantry division. The state of affairs in the lines of communication was deplorable, and the worst of it was that revolutionary propagandists were at work, not only behind the lines but at the front. The Intelligentzia rivalled the Japanese agents in their zeal for spreading disaffection amongst the troops. My son could not say enough in praise of the Japanese army. They were admirable in every way; but all the same we must persevere. We should get them in the end. Only he wondered what would happen afterwards. Whether we won or were beaten we should have civil war.

❖ The Vodka Monopoly During the Russo-Japanese War[1]

The vodka monopoly, as conceived by Alexander III, was essentially a measure intended to reduce the consumption of alcohol. In 1899, I travelled

1. From *The Memoirs of Count Witte* by Count Serge Witte. Copyright 1920, 1921 by Doubleday, a division of Bantam, Doubleday, Dell Publishing Group, Inc. Used by permission of Doubleday, a division of Bantam Doubleday Dell Publishing Group, Inc. pp. 56–57.

in the central provinces for the purpose of inspecting the work of introducing the vodka monopoly, which was going on there. In my talks with the officials I emphasized the fact that the reform was designed not to increase the State income, but to reduce the consumption of alcohol, and that the activity of the officials would be judged not by the amount of income derived by the State from the monopoly but by the beneficent effect of the measure upon the morals and health of the people. But when the Japanese war broke out and Kokovtzev became Minister of Finances, he completely distorted the meaning of the reform. Under the pressure of the huge war expenditures he began to treat the monopoly as a source of income for the State. To have the sale of vodka yield as large a profit as possible, was the sole purpose of his efforts in this direction. The amount of income derived from the monopoly became the measure of the worth of the excise officials. Not to restrict but to increase the consumption of vodka became the aim of the Government. Accordingly, no police measures were taken against drunkenness. The scale of prices was changed. The prices became high enough to ruin the habitual consumers, but not so high as the render the vodka inaccessible to the masses. The number of vodka shops was doubled. During the war there was some justification for this policy, but when the war was over it was the Minister's duty to remember the late Emperor's original purpose in carrying out his vodka reform.

✤ Bloody Sunday[1]

Gapon was a rather suspicious character. Some people said that he was a terrorist and others said that he was an *agent provocateur*. It has since been proved that he received considerable sums from the police department. He was sometimes pursued by the authorities and disappeared; at other times he would be going about the town quite openly to everybody's knowledge.

"So the priest Gapon has turned up again?" I asked.

"Yes. People are signing on with him to take part in the visit to the Czar."

"A visit to the Czar?"

"Yes. The Czar has invited all the workmen to come and see him. Some fair-minded men who are well disposed to us have informed him that the

1. Reprinted from Brian and Beatrix Lunn, co-trans. *The Memoirs of Baron N. Wrangel, 1847–1920*, pp. 214–218. Copyright 1927 by J. B. Lippincott Company, reprinted by permission of HarperCollins.

authorities are oppressing us and he wants to hear our own account of the matter.''

''My poor fellow, Gapon is deceiving you. You will land yourselves in a mess. The Czar will never receive you. The priest is leading you into a trap from which you will find it difficult to get out.''

He looked at me superciliously.

''It is obvious,'' he said, ''that the rich do not like the idea of the workers getting into touch with our father, the Czar. The Czar has invited us and we shall go, whatever you say.''

''If that is your attitude, I won't say any more. Go to him. It's your own business; but if one of you happens to be a ruffian who has wormed his way in amongst you and . . .''

''Oh, no, sir! Gapon is going to talk to them all first and tell them that they're not to carry any arms; and he is instructing everybody to wear their Sunday clothes. When you call on the Czar you must look your best.''

Work had started again, not only with us, but in all the factories; this was very odd. At this period one works or another was always on strike. Everybody in the town knew that a demonstration by the workers had been fixed for the 9th January.

The morning of the 9th I went to our factory; but after crossing the Neva I came back. A police officer told me that I could continue on my way, but that in all probability nobody would be allowed to come back from Vasilievsky Ostrov. Serious disorders were expected, and if they occurred, as they obviously would, communications would be cut.

An enormous crowd of workmen were in fact massed on the quay; but, as far as I could ascertain, they were just holiday-making and seemed to be perfectly peaceful. A large number of troops were on duty on the square of the Winter Palace, where the Emperor was in residence. It was only through the good offices of a colonel whom I knew, who was guarding the quadrant leading to the Morskaia with his regiment, that I was able to continue on my way. He told me that the soldiers had been supplied with ammunition.

''Why?'' I asked. '' Everything will go off perfectly all right; the Emperor will receive a deputation or show himself to the people from the balcony.''

''My dear fellow,'' he replied, ''where have you been all this time? Don't you know that His Majesty has left St. Petersburg?''

''Left St. Petersburg! When?''

''I'm not quite sure when he went away. Some people said he went yesterday; others assure me that it was several days ago.''

I was struck by his saying that the Emperor had been gone some days, for in that case I had been a witness of his ignominious departure.

One evening, at about seven, I was with a dealer who kept a shop in the Voznesenskaia, just opposite the big store. It was just before closing time and the street was full of people. Suddenly at racing speed a closed carriage drove up, rushing along like a fire engine. I thought at first that the horses had bolted; but it was obvious that the coachman was deliberately driving them at that speed, although it was against the regulations. Then I recognized the Emperor sitting right in the back of the carriage; and the crowd in the street had recognised him too. Urchins were whistling and shouting "Hallo, Hallo! Stop him! Stop thief!" The public were laughing, whistling and cheering. "The old boy has got the wind up," they were saying. And the carriage tore on at a furious pace towards the station. An old soldier, who was wearing the Cross of St. George was looking utterly dismayed.

"What a disgrace! What a disgrace!" he cried. "And it's the Czar. I saw his grandfather; he was really the Lord's Annointed!"

The whole world has heard of the massacre of the 9th January. The workers were formed up in perfect order. Singing psalms and the national anthem, "God save the Czar," they crossed the Neva and proceeded quietly towards the Emperor's residence. The priest Gapon, wearing priest's robes, marched at their head, carrying a cross. After him were men carrying holy images and the Emperor's portrait. When they had reached the palace the police ordered the procession to retire. The men halted. The order was given to disperse.

The crowd did not move and continued to sing their litanies.

The order was repeated three times and then . . . the massacre began.

The number of victims was never known.

The Intelligentzia said they numbered tens of thousands, the official authorities said they numbered about ten. In his Memoirs, Witte says, "There were more than two hundred," which is also rather a vague figure.

Why were such violent measures taken?

Two friends of mine who were generals on the Staff, and who were both men of the same type and men of judgment, had seen what happened from the same window, but their answers were quite different.

The one said: "It was impossible not to open fire; otherwise they would certainly have come into conflict with the troops. I am opposed to violent methods, but I should have given the order of fire myself."

"It was quite unnecessary," said the other. "During the Odessa riots I gave the order to fire too; but now nothing would induce me to do so."

It is impossible after this kind of thing to retain any faith in the views of eye-witnesses.

What I am certain about is that if His Majesty had shewn himself to the people, nothing would have happened, except that the Czar might have gained prestige. But the wretched man never knew how to make use of the opportunities that came his way.

This lamentable episode did much to ruin the last traces of Imperial prestige, and the people said:

"We, the Czar's children, used to tremble before our father; now our father, the Czar, trembles before his children and massacres them in terror."

✥ *The 1905 Revolution*[1]

A general feeling of profound discontent with the existing order was the most apparent symptom of the corruption with which the social and political life of Russia was infested. It was this feeling that united all the classes of the population. They all joined in a demand for radical political reforms, but the manner in which the different social groups visioned the longed-for changes varied with each class of people.

The upper classes, the nobility, were dissatisfied and impatient with the Government. They were not averse to the idea of limiting the Emperor's autocratic powers, but with a view to benefiting their own class. Their dream was an aristocratic constitutional monarchy. The merchants and captains of industry, the rich, looked forward to a constitutional monarchy of the bur-geois type and dreamed of the leadership of capital and of a mighty race of Russian Rothschilds. The "intelligentzia," i.e., members of various liberal professions, hoped for a constitutional monarchy, which was eventually to result in a bourgeois republic modelled upon the pattern of the French State. The students, not only in the universities, but in the advanced high school grades, recognized no law,—except the word of those who preached the most extreme revolutionary and anarchistic theories. Many of the officials in the various governmental bureaus were against the régime they served, for they were disgusted with the shameful system of corruption which had grown to such gigantic proportions during the reign of Nicholas II. The zem-stvo and municipal workers had long before declared that safety lay in the adoption of a constitution. As for the workmen, they were concerned about filling their stomachs with more food than had been their wont. For this rea-son they revelled in all manner of socialistic schemes of state organization. They fell completely under the sway of the revolutionists and rendered assis-tance without stint wherever there was need of physical force.

Finally, the majority of the Russian people, the peasantry, were anxious to increase their land holdings and to do away with the unrestrained arbi-trary actions on the part of the higher landed class and of the police through-out the extent of its hierarchy, from the lowest gendarme to the provincial governor. The peasant's dream was an autocratic Czar, but a people's Czar, pledged to carry out the principle proclaimed in the reign of Emperor Alex-ander II, to wit, the emancipation of the peasants with land in violation of the sacredness of property rights. The peasants were inclined to relish the

---

1. From *The Memoirs of Count Witte* by Count Serge Witte. Copyright 1920, 1921 by Doubleday, a division of Bantam, Doubleday, Dell Publishing Group, Inc. Used by permission of Doubleday, a division of Bantam Doubleday Dell Publishing Group, Inc. pp. 266–276.

idea of a constitutional monarchy and the socialistic principles as they were formulated by the labourite party, which party emphasized labour and the notion that labour alone, especially physical labour, is the foundation of all right. The peasants, too, were ready to resort to violence in order to obtain more land and, in general, to better their intolerable condition.

It is noteworthy that the nobility was willing to share the public pie with the middle class, but neither of these classes had a sufficiently keen eye to notice the appearance on the historical stage of a powerful rival, who was numerically superior to both and possessed the advantage of having nothing to lose. No sooner did this hitherto unnoticed class, the proletariat, approach the pie than it began to roar like a beast which stops at nothing to devour its prey . . . .

Anarchistic attacks directed against the lives of government officials; riots in all the institutions of higher learning and even in the secondary schools, which were accompanied by various excesses; trouble in the army; disturbances among peasants and workmen, involving destruction of property, personal injury and loss of life; and finally strikes,—such were the main conditions with which the authorities had to cope. On October 8, 1905, traffic on the railroads adjoining Moscow ceased completely. It took the railway strike but two days to spread to the Kharkov railroad junction, and on October 12th, the St. Petersburg junction was tied up. In the subsequent days traffic ceased on the remaining railroads. By October 17th, nearly the entire railway net and the telegraph were in a state of complete paralysis. About the same time almost all the factories and mills in the large industrial centres of Russia came to a stand-still. In St. Petersburg the strike in the factories and mills began on the 12th day of October, and on the 15th the business life of the capital was completely tied up. . . .

The city of St. Petersburg, the intellectual capital of the country, with its large industrial population was, naturally enough, one of the chief storm centres of the revolution: It was there that the council (*Soviet*) of Workmen's Deputies came into being. The idea of setting up this institution was born in the early days of October, and the press began to agitate for it among the working population of the capital. On October 13th, the first session of the Soviet took place in the Technological Institute. At this session an appeal was issued to the workmen of the capital, urging them to strike and to formulate extreme political demands. The second session took place in the same building the following day. At this session a certain Nosar, a Jew and an assistant attorney-at-law, was elected president of the Soviet. Nosar, for purposes of propaganda, worked as a weaver at Chesher's factory and was known there under the name of Khrustalev. The working population of St. Petersburg, almost in its entirety, carried out the decision of the Soviet with complete submission. On October 15th, the Soviet met again in the same building, this session being attended by several professors and a few members of other liberal professions, who took an active part in the discussions. The next day, in consequence of the publication of new rulings concerning public meetings, the school and university buildings were closed down. For this reason the Soviet could not meet that day. On October 17th, the Soviet held a session in the hall of the Free Economic Society. By that time it counted upward of two hundred members.

The historical manifesto which granted the country a constitution was issued on the 17th of October, 1905, and on the same day "The Bulletins (*Izviestiya*) of the Soviet of Workmen's Deputies," a purely revolutionary organ, began to be printed in turn in several printing houses. Needless to say, this was done in spite of the owners of the presses, who were far from being revolutionaries. . . .

The Workmen's Soviet met on October 18th and decided to declare a general strike, as an expression of the workmen's dissatisfaction with the manifesto. Nevertheless, the strike movement in Moscow and elsewhere began to wane and railroad traffic was soon restored to normal conditions. Under these circumstances the Soviet, at its session of October 19th, decided to call off the strike two days later. During the days following closely upon the publication of the manifesto, frequent clashes took place in the streets of the capital between the revolutionaries, on one side, and the troops, the police, and counter-revolutionaries, on the other. During these clashes, several people were killed and wounded. Among them was Professor Tarle, of the St. Petersburg University, who was wounded in the head, near the Technological Institute. The Soviet attempted to organize demonstrations in connection with the funeral of the fallen workmen, but the Government did not permit it. After October 17th, I gave orders to allow all peaceful processions arranged in connection with the manifesto, but to suppress the demonstrations at the first sign of disorder and violation of the public peace. The demonstration which was to accompany the funeral was clearly intended to cause disorder and consequently was not permitted.

Generally speaking, several days after October 17th St. Petersburg quieted down, and throughout the six months of my premiership I did not enact a single extraordinary measure relating to the administration of St. Petersburg and its district. Nor was there a single case of capital punishment. All the extraordinary measures were taken later, when Stolypin inaugurated the policy of undoing the reform of October 17th. . . .

Elsewhere in Russia, however, the demonstrations connected with the manifesto were accompanied by disorders. Thus, for instance, on October 26th, riots broke out at Kronstadt. They were not quelled until October 28th. Kronstadt, a city administered by the Ministry of the Navy, was revolutionary to an extraordinary degree. The spirit of revolt was rooted deeper among the sailors than in the army. Even before October 17th, this spirit manifested itself in military pronunciamentos among the sailors at Sevastopol and partly at Nikolayev and Kronstadt. This revolutionary spirit became rampant among the sailors because of the naval authorities' misrule and also because the sailors were recruited from the more intelligent elements of the population, which fall an easier prey to revolutionary propaganda. It must be borne in mind that in those days the revolutionizing process was going on among vast masses of people.

The publication of the manifesto gave rise to numerous joyful demonstrations all over the country. They were met by counter-demonstrations conducted by bands known as Black Hundreds. These bands, which were so nicknamed because of their small numbers, were made up of hooligans. But as they were supported in some places by the local authorities, they soon began to grow in number and weight, and then it all ended in a pogrom directed mostly, it not exclusively, against the Jews. Furthermore, as the extreme Left elements were also dissatisfied with the manifesto because of its insufficient radicalism and also indulged in rioting without meeting sufficient moral opposition on the part of the liberals, the hooligans of the Right, that is, the Black Hundreds, soon found support in the central administration and then also higher up.

In connection with the Department of Police a printing press was set up for turning out pogrom proclamations intended to incite the dark masses mostly against the Jews. This activity, to which I put an end, was revealed to me by the former Director of the Police Department, Lopukhin, who is now in exile in Siberia. But in the provinces this activity was going on as before. Thus, in my premiership a pogrom was perpetrated against the Jews at Homel. The riot was provoked by the gendarmerie. When I discovered this shameful incident, and reported it to the Council of Ministers, His Majesty wrote on the memorandum about this affair that such matters should not be brought to his attention (as too trivial a subject). . . . The Emperor must have been influenced in this case by the Minister of the Interior, Durnovo.

After the strike was over, beginning October 27th, the workmen in several mills started to introduce by direct action the eight-hour workday. The Workmen's Soviet took advantage of the situation and decreed the forceful introduction of the eight-hour day. The Soviet felt that it was losing its prestige among the workmen. On November 1st it called a second general strike, emphasizing the necessity of this measure as a protest against the introduction of marital law in Poland and also against the manner in which the Government suppressed the riots at Kronstadt. I learned about this step that same night and I wired at once to the workers of several mills, warning them to cease obeying persons who, clearly, were leading them to ruin and starvation. In my dispatch I told the workers that I was advising them in a spirit of comradeship. The phrase was rather unusual in the mouth of the head of the Government addressing the workmen. Some of the newspapers, *Novoye Vremya* included, took up the phrase and began to make sport of it. On the other hand, the labour leaders, touched to the quick by the influence my dispatch exerted upon the workers, grew furious. Nevertheless, the strike proved a failure, the workmen ceased to obey the Soviet and their leaders, and, therefore, on the 5th of November the Soviet decided to call off the strike. Generally speaking, the strikes were over by November 7th, and the Emperor wrote to me on that same day: "I am glad that this senseless railroad strike is over. This is a great moral triumph for the Government."

On November 13th, the Soviet again considered the proposition of declaring a general strike. The plan was rejected, and the Soviet was also constrained "temporarily" to discontinue the forceful introduction of the eight-hour workday. From that time on the authority of the Soviet began rapidly to decline and its organization to decay. It was then that I found it opportune to have Nosar arrested. The arrest was made on November 26th. Thereupon the Soviet elected a præsidium of three to replace Nosar. This præsidium held secret sessions, while the body of the Soviet did not meet at all. I had intended to have Nosar arrested at an earlier date, but Litvinoff-Falinski, now in charge of one of the departments of the Chief Management of Commerce and Industry, persuaded me to refrain from so doing. He argued that it was necessary to postpone the arrest till the workmen would welcome it, that is, until Nosar and the Soviet would have lost all prestige. In this fashion we would avoid an unnecessary clash with the workmen, a clash which might prove bloody. This was judicious advice. After Nosar was taken, I ordered the arrest of the whole Soviet, which order Durnovo carried out on December 3rd. Durnovo feared that the members would disperse and escape if he started arresting them separately. He therefore waited for the Soviet to meet, which the latter hesitated to do. Their fears were well founded, for as soon as the body gathered on December 3rd in the Hall of the Free Economic Society, the members, 190 in all, were rounded up and arrested. After Nosar's arrest the Soviet had attempted to put through a plan for a general strike as a protest against the arrest, but their efforts were in vain.

Thus ended the affair of the Workmen's Soviet and its leader, Nosar. The matter was greatly overdrawn by the press, for the simple reason that these strikes, involving, as they did, the printers, touched the pockets of the newspaper people. Of course, there were among the journalists men who sympathized with the "Workers' Revolution," but those of impecunious journalists, mostly dreamers. Revolution always and everywhere brings forth such fanatical idealists.

✢ *Witte's "Loan That Saved Russia"*[1]

My next great task was to secure a foreign loan. As early as 1904 the need for a foreign loan became apparent. At that time our financial system was already giving way under the pressure of the war expenditures. In conclud-

1. From *The Memoirs of Count Witte* by Count Serge Witte. Copyright 1920, 1921 by Doubleday, a division of Bantam, Doubleday, Dell Publishing Group, Inc. Used by permission of Doubleday, a division of Bantam Doubleday Dell Publishing Group, Inc. pp. 292, 296–297, 304–305, 307–308.

ing our second commercial treaty with Germany in 1904, I succeeded in securing Germany's permission to float our loan in that country. The next year I made an effort to prepare the ground for the loan in France and in the United States, where I went on the Portsmouth peace mission. My intention was to conclude the loan before the opening of the Imperial Duma. As I felt sure that the first Duma would be unbalanced and to a certain extent revengeful, I was afraid that its interference might thwart the loan negotiations and render the bankers less tractable. As a result, the Government, without funds, would lose the freedom of action which is so essential during a period of upheaval.

In January, 1906, I decided to push further the negotiations for the loan, which I had initiated in Paris on my way back from the United States. As I could not go abroad and as there was no one who could be entrusted with the task of conducting the negotiations, I asked Neutzlin to come to Russia. It was a matter of extreme importance that his visit should be a secret to the public, for otherwise it would have had an undesirable effect upon the course of the Algeciras Conference and upon the Russian Stock Exchange. I may mention in passing that since I had left the post of Minister of Finances, in 1903, the Russian securities had fallen twenty per cent. Accordingly, Neutzlin came to Russia incognito and put up at the palace of Grand Duke Vladimir Alexandrovich, at Tsarskoye Selo. He arrived on February 2nd, and his visit lasted five days. In the course of that period I had several conferences with Neutzlin, and the presence of the Minister of Finance, Shipov, we agreed upon the terms of the loan. At first, Neutzlin insisted that the loan should not be realized before the opening of the Duma, but I succeeded in convincing him of the undesirability of such an arrangement, and it was then agreed that the loan should be effected immediately upon the termination of the Algeciras Conference. It was also agreed that the amount of the loan should be made as large as possible, so as to enable us to get along for a considerable period of time without new loans and also in order to cancel the temporary loans contracted by Kokovtzev in France and in Germany. I insisted on 2,750,000,000 francs as the nominal amount of the loan. Anticipating upon the course of events, I may say that, owing to the treachery of Germany and of the American syndicate of bankers headed by Morgan, we had to reduce the amount to 2,250,000,000 francs—843,750,000 rubles. Neutzlin insisted on six and a quarter per cent, but I could not agree to that rate of interest, and it was fixed at six per cent, the loan certificates becoming convertible after ten years. The syndicate which was to handle the loan was to be made up, we agreed, of French, Dutch, English, German, American, and Russian banking firms. Austrian banks were also permitted to participate in the loan. The sums realized were to be left in the hands of the syndicate at one and a quarter per cent and then transferred to the Russian Government in definite installments in the course of one year. Not less than half of the amount of the loan the syndicate was to take upon itself. . . .

Thus, Germany first protracted the Algeciras Conference in the hope that, unable to contract a loan, we would cease the free exchange of credit notes for gold. Germany would have greatly profited thereby, for Russia would then be at the mercy of Berlin stock exchange speculation, as was the case before I introduced the gold standard. She failed, however, to reach her goal. Then at the last moment, on the very eve of the conclusion of the loan, she treacherously ordered her bankers to refrain from participation in that transaction. Morgan followed suit and also refused to participate in the loan. That American banker enjoyed the German Emperor's favour, and despite his democratic feelings as an American, highly valued the attention of that exalted crowned personage. . . .

The refusal of the Germans and Americans to participate in the loan had no effect on the English. Neutzlin sent me a telegram to that effect immediately upon Fischel's declaration. The Algeciras affair was the first manifestation in many years of a growing rapprochement between Russia and England. At the Conference Russia and Great Britain showed the world an example of complete solidarity in giving their full support to France. Nor did the Austrian banks withdraw. Italy did refuse to participate, but for purely financial reasons. She had just succeeded in stabilizing her financial system. Several years ago the Italian king, while on a stay in Russia, presented me with an Italian gold coin, saying that he had brought me the first gold coin struck at the Italian mint, as a fitting gift to the man who introduced the gold standard in the great Russian empire. . . .

It appears from this letter of the most prominent German banker that this time, too, the German Government had missed fire. In fact, as early as April 17th (30th) Neutzlin, the chief representative of the syndicate, wrote me as follows:

> The international loan is an accomplished fact. The last stage was reached yesterday. This great financial victory is to-day the subject of general conversation, and Russian credit, for the first time since the beginning of the war, is in the process of striking root in a considerably enlarged territory. Having reported this triumph, to which, thanks to your Excellency, I have had the honor of contributing my share from first to last, I turn to your Excellency filled with profound gratefulness for the confidence you have shown me throughout the course of the negotiations. In abandoning, in the course of our conversation at Tsarskoye Selo, the plans prepared beforehand, your Excellency gave me the full measure of your approval, which alone sustained and encouraged me during the critical stages which the negotiations traversed.

The loan was indeed an achievement of the highest importance. It was the largest foreign loan in the history of the modern nations. After the Franco-Prussian War, Thiers succeeded in securing a somewhat greater loan, but it was largely an internal loan, while this one was almost exclusively subscribed abroad. By means of it Russia maintained intact its gold standard of currency, which I introduced in 1896. This, in its turn, served to sustain all the basic principles of our financial system, which were mostly inaugurated by myself, and which Kokovtzev preserved with laudable firmness. It was these principles that enabled Russia to recover after that ill-starred war and the subsequent senseless turmoil, known as the Russian revolution. This loan enabled the Imperial Government to weather all the vicissitudes of the period extending from 1906 to 1910 by providing it with funds, which together with the troops recalled from Transbaikalia restored consistency and assurance to the acts of the Government.

✤ *Stolypin's Land Reform*[1]

During the period of reaction which followed the assassination of Alexander II, the *obshchina* continued to be the pet of the Minister of the Interior, but the civil rights of the peasants were considerably curtailed. The revolution found the peasants in a very lamentable state. The collective form of land ownership was still prevalent among them, and the burden of legal disabilities weighed down upon them heavily. Legally the peasant was not of age, so to speak. While no longer the landowner's serf, he was still the serf of the rural administration, and above all of the rural chief of police.

When I became Minister of Finances my acquaintance with the peasant problem was very superficial. For a time I was inclined to accept the Slavophils' view of *obshchina,* for the teachings of those great idealists have always swayed my heart. Contact with reality and the influence of ex-Minister of Finances Bunge, who was a resolute enemy of the *obshchina,* increased my interest in the peasant problem and gave a different direction to my views on the subject. Before long, I perceived that the mediæval *obshchina* was a serious hindrance to the economic development of the country. In order to raise the productivity of peasant labour it was necessary, I found, besides removing the legal disabilities of the peasant class, to make the product of labour the full and assured property of the toiler and his heirs. No efficiency or initiative can be developed as long as the peasant knows that the land he tills may be given away to another member of the commune; that the fruit of his labour will be divided not on the basis of common law, but in conformity with custom, which is often the synonym of arbitrary dis-

---

1. From the *Memoirs of Count Witte* by Count Serge Witte. Copyright 1920, 1921 by Doubleday, a division of Bantam, Doubleday, Dell Publishing Group, Inc. Used by permission of Doubleday, a division of Bantam Doubleday Dell Publishing Group, Inc. pp. 387–389.

posal; that he is responsible for the taxes unpaid by his neighbours, and, finally, that he is at the mercy of the rural chief of police.

The improvement of the legal and economic status of the peasant was one of my main preoccupations since the very beginning of the reign of Emperor Nicholas II. All my efforts to abolish the redemption payments during my administration of the Ministry of Finances proved unavailing ("Why indulge the muzhik?"), and it was only after the act of October 17th, 1905, that I succeeded in enacting this measure. A considerable extension of the operations of the Peasant Bank was another step toward a betterment of the peasant's condition, which was made by my Cabinet. We did not think it advisable to go further without placing the matter before the newly created legislative body, which was soon to convene. We also established a chain of local committees for the study of agrarian conditions and we elaborated a program of peasant reforms to be submitted to the Duma. Individual land ownership and full legal rights for the peasant class were the two basic principles of that program. The transition from communal to individual land ownership was to be gradual and free from all compulsion.

Stolypin's Cabinet and the third Duma took advantage of the legislative plan which we had laid, but in doing so they distorted them to such an extent that the land reform which is now being carried out may lead to grave revolutionary complications. Like myself, Stolypin intended to develop a class of small private landowners from among the peasants, but with his characteristic faith in the efficacy of coercion he inaugurated a policy of forcefully disrupting the time-hallowed institution of the *obshchina*. Besides, while forcing upon the peasant individual land ownership, the new law (Act of November 9, 1906) failed to grant him full civic rights, notably the right of inheritance. The reform is being carried out hastily and ill-advisedly, without paying due attention to the secondary problems raised by it, as if it were a mere police measure and not an act of overwhelming national importance. Its only outcome will be a chaotic condition in the village and rapid proletarization of the peasant masses.

By his arbitrary, deceitful and brutal actions Stolypin aroused against himself a considerable part of the population. No other statesman has ever succeeded in drawing upon himself the enmity of so many men and women. For instance, all the non-Russian national groups of the Empire were among his enemies. Furthermore, Stolypin lost the respect of all decent people. Through his double dealing he estranged the very Black Hundred leaders who were his main support during the first years of his premiership. Under these circumstances it was easy enough to foresee that he would come to grief. It was clear to me that since he stubbornly clung to his post, he would perish at it. To what extent my presentiment was definite may be seen from the following fact. When Dillon, the well-known English journalist, visited me at Biarritz and inquired about conditions in Russia, my reply was to the effect that some fatal catastrophe was bound to happen to Stolypin and produce a general change in the political situation.

My foreboding came true. On September 1, 1911, Stolypin was fatally wounded. The attempt took place at Kiev during a solemn theatrical performance attended by the Emperor, his daughters, all the Cabinet Ministers and a great many members of the high aristocracy. The shooting was done by a revolutionary terrorist who was at the same time a Secret Service agent. Several days later Stolypin died. The Emperor bestowed a number of favours upon the widow, while the jingoist papers mourned Stolypin's death as Russia's great loss, and opened subscription funds for the construction of a national chain of memorial statutes. Of course, this artificial agitation soon subsided and gave place to a sober estimate of the late Minister's historical rôle.

✤ *Stolypin on Population Growth*[1]

We must no longer tie laborers to the land nor allot from their portions to relieve over-population in other labor districts. Consider figures on the population increase for a ten year period in the fifty provinces of European Russia. Russians, gentlemen, are not becoming extinct. Our population growth has surpassed the increase in all other countries of the world, reaching a figure of 15.1 per 1000 population annually. Thus, European Russia alone, in its fifty provinces, has increased by 1,625,000 persons a year in natural growth, or, considering a family to be five persons, 341,000 families. To satisfy the land needs of the accrued population alone, at 10 desiatines per household, would necessitate adding 3.5 million desiatines annually.

---

1. Reprinted from Maria Petrovna Von Bock, Margaret Patoski, ed. and trans. *Reminiscences of My Father, Peter A. Stolypin* (Metuchen, N.J. The Scarecrow Press, 1970), pp. 294–295.

✤ *Rasputin in St. Petersburg*[1]

His fate was decided by a chance meeting with a young missionary-monk, a well-informed, deeply religious man, as pure and as naïve as a child.

---

1. Reprinted from Prince Felix Youssoupoff, *Rasputin* (New York, Lincoln Mac Veagh/The Dial Press, 1927), pp. 34–35.

He believed in Rasputin's sincerity, and presented him to Bishop Theophan, who, in his turn, brought the imposter to St. Petersburg.

Any ordinary peasant would have become confused by life in the capital. He would have lost himself in the intricate web of Court, society and official relations.

No ordinary *muzhik* would have had the courage, particularly while everything was as yet strange to him, to show such ease and independence in such surroundings.

Incidentally, the easy manner and familiar tone which this former horse-stealer adopted even towards the most highly-placed personages, was a very considerable factor in his success. Rasputin went in and out of the Tsar's palace as calmly and unconstrainedly as if it had been his own cottage at Pokrovskoe. This made a deep impression. People were apt to think that nothing short of real saintliness could cause a simple Siberian peasant to show no sign whatever of servility before an earthly power. But this *muzhik* was not slow to observe, remember and turn in his mind everything that was of use to him in the noisy and crowded capital.

He almost flawlessly analysed certain characters, quickly perceiving the weak points of those whom he desired to influence, and adapting himself to them.

✥ *The Secret Telegram Sent by the Russian Ambassador in France, Izvolsky, to the Russian Foreign Secretary, Sazonov*[1]

Paris, July 14/27, 1914

Immediately upon my return to Paris, I saw the Minister of Justice [Bienvenu-Martin] in the presence of Abel Ferry and Berthelot. They confirmed the details of the steps taken by the German Ambassador, of which you have been informed by Sevastopoulo's telegrams Nos. 187 and 188. This morning, Baron Schoen confirmed in writing the declaration made by him yesterday, to wit:

---

1. Reprinted from Brian Tierney, Donald Kagan, and L. Pearce Williams, eds. *The Outbreak of World War I—Who Was Responsible?* (New York, Random House, 1977), pp. 32–33.

1. "Austria has declared to Russia that she is not seeking territorial acquisitions and will respect the integrity of Serbia. Her only aim is to assure her own security;
2. "The prevention of war consequently rests upon Russia;
3. "Germany and France entirely united in the ardent desire to maintain peace, ought to press Russia to be moderate."

The [French] Minister of Justice has told me that he does not understand the sense of the new proposal of Baron Schoen, but that he viewed it with defiance and proposed to tell him tomorrow that a reply would be given him on the return to Paris of the Minister of Foreign Affairs on Wednesday. Altogether, I am struck by the way the Minister of Justice and his colleagues correctly understand the situation and how firm and calm is their decision to give us the most complete support and to avoid the least appearance of divergence of view between us.

Izvolsky.

✛ Nicholas II on the Outbreak of the First World War: His Remarks to the Duma Members and the State Council in the Winter Palace (August 8, 1914)[1]

I greet you in these momentous, alarming days through which all Russia is passing.

First Germany, and then Austria, has declared war on Russia.

The tremendous outburst of patriotic feeling, love of country, and devotion to the Throne which has swept Our whole country like a hurricane, serves in My sight and, I trust, in yours, too, as a pledge that Our great Mother Russia will carry to the desired conclusion the war which the Lord God has sent her.

From this unanimous impulse of love and readiness for any sacrifice, even of life itself, I derive sustaining strength and the ability to look calmly and confidently towards the future.

---

1. Reprinted from Frank Alfred Golder, ed. and Emanuel Aronsberg, trans.
Documents of Russian History, 1914–1917 (New York, The Century Company, 1927), pp. 30–31.

We are not only defending Our honor and dignity within Our Own country, but are fighting as well for Our Slav brothers, who are one with Us in blood and faith.

And at this moment I see with joy, also, that the union of the Slavs with all of Russia is strengthened and indissoluble.

I feel convinced that all of you, each in his own sphere, will help Me bear the trial visited upon Me, and that each of Us, beginning with Myself, will fulfil his duty to the end.

Great is the God of Russia.

✤ *Domestic Difficulties in War Time: A Police Report (October 14–November 14, 1916)*[1]

In the opinion of the spokesmen of the labour group of the Central War Industries Committee, the industrial proletariat of the capital is on the verge of despair, and it believes that the smallest outbreak, due to any pretext, will lead to uncontrollable riots, with thousands and tens of thousands of victims. Indeed, the stage for such outbreaks is more than set: the economic position of the masses, in spite of the immense increase in wages, is distressing. . . . Even if we assume that wages have increased 100 per cent, the cost of living has risen by an average of 300 per cent. The impossibility of obtaining, even for cash, many foodstuffs and articles of prime necessity, the waste of time involved in spending hours waiting in line in front of stores, the increasing morbidity due to inadequate diet and anti-sanitary lodgings (cold and dampness as a result of lack of coal and firewood), etc.—all these conditions have created such a situation that the mass of industrial workers are quite ready to let themselves go to the wildest excesses of a hunger riot. . . .

---

1. Reprinted from R. J. Minney, *Rasputin* (London, Cassell and Company, LTD, 1972), p. 186.

✤ An Eye-Witness to Anti-Tsarist Soldiers Marching in Petrograd[1]

On the 1st March, when I got up my servant told me that some troops were arriving. I look out of the window and I thought I was dreaming. The houses were covered from top to bottom with red bunting. A large and orderly crowd, wearing red buttonholes, were lining the pavements. Huge red placards were borne in front of the regiments, the battalions and the platoons. A huge crowd, wearing red ties, stood on the pavement. The reflection of all this red colour, red houses, red scarves, red flags, red placards, made the whole street look red, as though it had been painted in blood.

Eighty thousand men, the whole military strength of the capital, were on their way to swear fidelity to the Revolution, just as, a little while since, they had taken the oath of allegiance to the Emperor, who was still on the throne and did not abdicate until some days later.

At the head of these red troops marched the former marines of the Imperial Guard, now become the Red Militia, "the pride and glory of the Revolution." Under a red scarf, with a red favour on his chest, marched its chief, an admiral, an aide-de-camp to His Majesty, a cousin of the Emperor, His Imperial Highness the Grand Duke Cyrille, who to-day has the audacity to declare himself the legitimate heir to the Czar's throne.

I should add that all these so-called Guards regiments were reserves. The genuine Guards were at the front, fighting the enemy. Those who were marching past under the red flag were simply reserve units attached to the regiments consisting of men who had just been mobilised. The real Guards remained loyal up to the moment when the Emperor himself absolved them from the oath of allegiance which they had taken.

---

1. Reprinted from Brian and Beatrix Lunn, co-trans. *The Memoirs of Baron N. Wrangel, 1847–1920,* pp. 274–275. Copyright 1927 by J. B. Lippincott Company, reprinted by permission of HarperCollins.

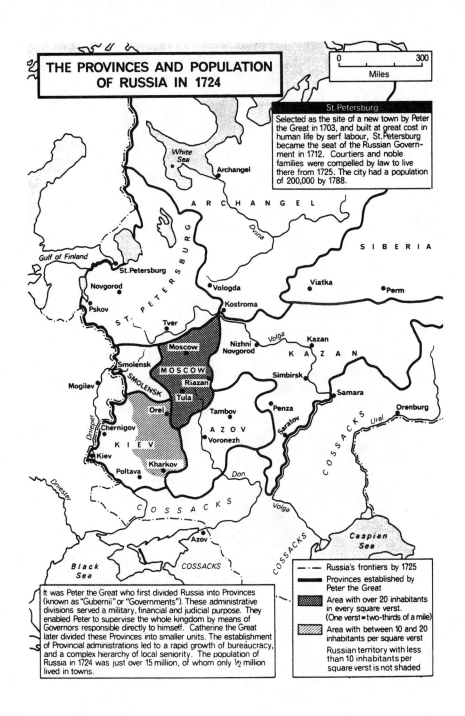

THE PROVINCES AND POPULATION OF RUSSIA IN 1724

0   300
Miles

St. Petersburg

Selected as the site of a new town by Peter the Great in 1703, and built at great cost in human life by serf labour, St. Petersburg became the seat of the Russian Government in 1712. Courtiers and noble families were compelled by law to live there from 1725. The city had a population of 200,000 by 1788.

White Sea

Archangel

A R C H A N G E L

Dvina

S I B E R I A

Gulf of Finland

St. Petersburg

S T · P E T E R S B U R G

Novgorod

Vologda

Viatka

Perm

Pskov

Kostroma

Tver

Nizhni Novgorod

Volga

Kazan

K A Z A N

Moscow

M O S C O W

Smolensk

SMOLENSK

Riazan

Simbirsk

Mogilev

Tula

Samara

Orel

Chernigov

K I E V

Tambov

A Z O V

Voronezh

Penza

Saratov

Orenburg

Ural

C O S S A C K S

Kiev

Kharkov

Poltava

Don

Dnieper

Dniester

C O S S A C K S

Volga

Azov

COSSACKS

C O S S A C K S

Caspian Sea

Black Sea

It was Peter the Great who first divided Russia into Provinces (known as "Gubernii" or "Governments"). These administrative divisions served a military, financial and judicial purpose. They enabled Peter to supervise the whole kingdom by means of Governors responsible directly to himself. Catherine the Great later divided these Provinces into smaller units. The establishment of Provincial administrations led to a rapid growth of bureaucracy, and a complex hierarchy of local seniority. The population of Russia in 1724 was just over 15 million, of whom only ½ million lived in towns.

- – · – Russia's frontiers by 1725
- ▬▬ Provinces established by Peter the Great
- Area with over 20 inhabitants in every square verst. (One verst = two-thirds of a mile)
- Area with between 10 and 20 inhabitants per square verst
- Russian territory with less than 10 inhabitants per square verst is not shaded

RUSSIAN EXPANSION UNDER CATHERINE THE GREAT 1762–1796

The Provinces of Russia in 1750

Territory annexed by Russia 1762–1796, giving Russia an outlet on the Black Sea, and a common frontier with Prussia and Austria

White Sea

Archangel

ARCHANGEL

FINLAND

Helsingfors

ESTONIA

ST. PETERSBURG

Novgorod

NOVGOROD

Vologda

Viatka

Perm

LIVONIA

Pskov

Baltic Sea

KURLAND

Tver

MOSCOW

KAZAN

Kazan

Ufa

UFA

Niemen

Vilna

LITHUANIA

Minsk

SMOLENSK

Moscow

NIZHNI NOVGOROD

PRUSSIA

WHITE RUSSIA

Stavropol

Samara

Warsaw

Pinsk

Orel

AUSTRIA

PODLESIA

Lutsk

KIEV

Kiev

BELGOROD

VORONEZH

Dnieper

Belgorod

Dniester

PODOLIA

ZAPOROZHE

ASTRAKHAN

Jassy

Odessa

Taganrog

Astrakhan

Caspian Sea

CRIMEA

KUBAN

Kutchuk Kainardji

Sebastopol

KABARDA

Tarki

Black Sea

Constantinople

THE OTTOMAN EMPIRE

Kars

0   200
Miles

PERSIA

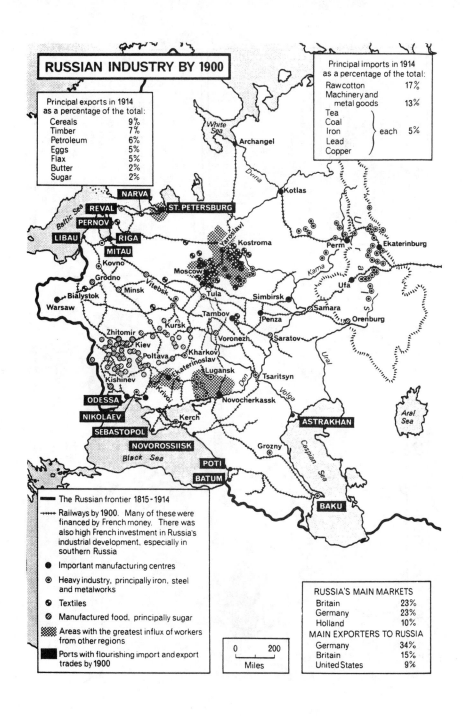

RUSSIAN INDUSTRY BY 1900

Principal imports in 1914
as a percentage of the total:

Raw cotton	17%
Machinery and metal goods	13%
Tea	
Coal	
Iron	each 5%
Lead	
Copper	

Principal exports in 1914
as a percentage of the total:

Cereals	9%
Timber	7%
Petroleum	6%
Eggs	5%
Flax	5%
Butter	2%
Sugar	2%

White Sea

Archangel

Dvina

Kotlas

NARVA

REVAL

PERNOV

ST. PETERSBURG

Yaroslavl

Kostroma

Perm

Ekaterinburg

LIBAU

RIGA

MITAU

Kovno

Moscow

Kama

Ufa

Baltic Sea

Grodno

Vitebsk

Minsk

Tula

Simbirsk

Samara

Orenburg

Bialystok

Warsaw

Kursk

Tambov

Penza

Saratov

Ural

Zhitomir

Kiev

Voronezh

Poltava

Kharkov

Ekaterinoslav

Lugansk

Tsaritsyn

Kishinev

Krivoi

Don

Novocherkassk

Volga

Aral Sea

ODESSA

NIKOLAEV

Kerch

ASTRAKHAN

SEBASTOPOL

NOVOROSSIISK

Black Sea

Grozny

Caspian Sea

POTI

BATUM

BAKU

— The Russian frontier 1815-1914

┅ Railways by 1900. Many of these were financed by French money. There was also high French investment in Russia's industrial development, especially in southern Russia

● Important manufacturing centres

◉ Heavy industry, principally iron, steel and metalworks

◉ Textiles

⊘ Manufactured food, principally sugar

▓ Areas with the greatest influx of workers from other regions

▬ Ports with flourishing import and export trades by 1900

0   200
Miles

RUSSIA'S MAIN MARKETS

Britain	23%
Germany	23%
Holland	10%

MAIN EXPORTERS TO RUSSIA

Germany	34%
Britain	15%
United States	9%

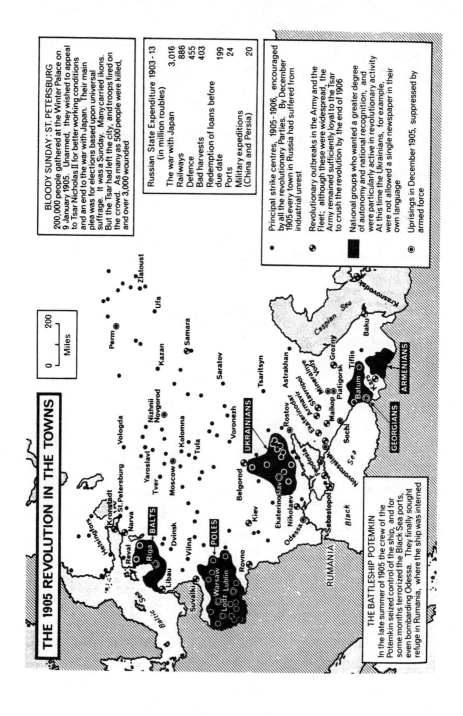

THE 1905 REVOLUTION IN THE TOWNS

BLOODY SUNDAY : ST. PETERSBURG
200,000 people gathered at the Winter Palace on 9 January 1905. Unarmed, they wished to appeal to Tsar Nicholas II for better working conditions and an end to the war with Japan. Their main plea was for elections based upon universal suffrage. It was a Sunday. Many carried ikons. But the Tsar had left the city, and troops fired on the crowd. As many as 500 people were killed, and over 3,000 wounded

Russian State Expenditure 1903 - 13 (in million roubles)	
The war with Japan	3,016
Railways	886
Defence	455
Bad harvests	403
Redemption of loans before due date	199
Ports	24
Military expeditions (China and Persia)	20

- Principal strike centres, 1905 - 1906, encouraged by all the revolutionary Parties. By December 1905 every town in Russia had suffered from industrial unrest

- Revolutionary outbreaks in the Army and the Fleet; although these were widespread, the Army remained sufficiently loyal to the Tsar to crush the revolution by the end of 1906

- National groups who wanted a greater degree of autonomy and national recognition, and were particularly active in revolutionary activity. At this time the Ukrainians, for example, were not allowed a single newspaper in their own language

- Uprisings in December 1905, suppressed by armed force

THE BATTLESHIP POTEMKIN
In the late summer of 1905 the crew of the Potemkin seized control of the ship, and for some months terrorized the Black Sea ports, even bombarding Odessa. They finally sought refuge in Rumania, where the ship was interned

0   200
Miles

Zlatoust
Ufa
Perm
Samara
Kazan
Saratov
Vologda
Yaroslavl
Nizhnii Novgorod
Kolomna
Tver
Moscow
Tula
Voronezh
Tsaritsyn
Astrakhan
Helsingfors
Kronstadt
St. Petersburg
Narva
BALTS
Reval
Riga
Dvinsk
Libau
Vilna
Suvalki
Warsaw
Lodz   Lublin
POLES
Rovno
Kiev
Belgorod
Ekaterinoslav
UKRAINIANS
Nikolaev
Odessa
Sebastopol
RUMANIA
Black Sea
Novorossisk
Rostov
Ekaterinodar
Maikop
Mineralnye Vody
Stavropol
Armavir
Sochi
Batum
GEORGIANS
Tiflis
ARMENIANS
Grozny
Piatigorsk
Baku
Caspian Sea
Krasnovodsk
Baltic Sea

RUSSIA, THE BALKANS, AND THE COMING OF WAR 1912–1914

0 ___ 500

Miles

North Sea

BRITAIN

Baltic

St. Petersburg

Reval

Riga

BALTIC PROVINCES

Moscow

RUSSIA

Danzig

Berlin

Warsaw

Pripet Marshes

GERMANY

Breslau

POLISH PROVINCES

VOLHYNIA

Kiev

Paris

Lemberg

FRANCE

Vienna

Budapest

AUSTRIA - HUNGARY

BOSNIA

Sarajevo

Belgrade

RUMANIA

Black Sea

SERBIA

BULGARIA

Constantinople

MONTENEGRO

ALBANIA

Bosphorus

GREECE

Dardanelles

TURKEY

Adriatic Sea

Russia's mid-century alignment with Germany was changed during the 1880's to a new alignment with France, while at the same time Austria and Germany drew closer together. In the two Balkan Wars of 1912 and 1913 Turkey was driven almost entirely from Europe, but Russia's position did not improve; for as a result of Turkey's defeat Austrian influence increased even further. In June 1914 a Bosnian Serb murdered the Austrian heir to the throne, Archduke Franz-Ferdinand, at Sarajevo. Austria invaded Serbia on 28 July 1914. Russia then declared war on Austria. Germany supported her ally Austria and declared war on Russia. France and Britain joined Russia against Germany and Austria. Turkey attacked Russia in October 1914

Countries in which Austrian and German influence worked against Russia. Greece had a pro-German King; Turkey a pro-German Minister of War and virtual dictator; Bulgaria and Rumania had both accepted alliance with the Central Powers

Area of Russia in which Germany hoped to expand as a result of war

Russia's only two Balkan Allies, both threatened by Austria. Austria had created the state of Albania in 1912 in order to cut Serbia off from the sea.

Countries in western Europe sympathetic to Russia. France had a military alliance with Russia dating from 1894. Britain a convention dating from 1907

Questions to Consider

Although framed in an interrogative manner, these questions do not necessarily have one specific answer. Many of them are invitations for reflection and evaluation, and it is anticipated that they will assist in developing the capacity for historical thought.

Section One. Russian History in the Eighteenth Century

1. Why was Peter the Great personally interested in ship-building technology?
2. How much power did Peter give to the Senate?
3. On the basis of Korb's observations, assess the role of religion in the life of the Russian people.
4. What role did foreign and Russian courtiers play as power brokers during the reigns of Anna and Elizabeth, according to Manstein?
5. Voltaire referred to Asiatic aspects of Russian life, while in the *Nakaz* Catherine the Great called Russia a European power. Why did they differ? Who made the more accurate assessment?
6. What Enlightenment ideals are expressed in the *Nakaz*?
7. What was the position of the nobility during Catherine's reign, as described in the *Manifesto on the Freedom of the Nobility* and the *Charter of Rights*?
8. What was Catherine's goal in revamping the administrative organization of the empire?
9. Explain the significance of the Pugachev Revolt, in terms of the underlying causes and the specific challenges to Catherine's government which were raised.
10. Is there an indication that the three strong female rulers of Russia (Anna, Elizabeth, Catherine) attempted to improve the position of Russian women during their reigns? Why or why not?
11. The wealth of the nobility depended on the productive capacities of the peasants. Why were the peasants so poorly treated, as described in Radishchev's passage?
12. Czartoryski reports on a new elaborate ritual devised for the nobles by Paul. Some commentators ascribe this to mental instability. Do you think that there was a method to his madness?

Section Two. Russian History in the Nineteenth and Early Twentieth Centuries

1. How successful was Alexander I in reforming Russian government? Could he have gone farther? Why or why not?

2. What were the educational reforms of Alexander designed to achieve? Were they democratic in nature or did they aim to create a highly-trained group of specialists and experts?

3. Why was Napoleon defeated in Russia? What role was played by the common people, according to the London Times and the Earl of Liverpool?

4. What were the goals of the Decembrists? Were they actually revolutionaries?

5. Explain the position of the Russian nobility during the reign of Nicholas I, as described by Golovine.

6. How did the conflict over the shrines reveal the conflicting imperial claims of Russia and France?

7. What made the experience of the soldiers at the front in the Crimean War different from that of soldiers in the Napoleonic invasion of Russia?

8. What did Alexander II mean when he stated that it was better to emancipate the serfs from above than wait for such change to come from below?

9. What were the principal conditions of the Emancipation Manifesto, as summarized in the London Times? How was the relationship between landlord and peasant altered?

10. Describe the significance and function of the *mir*, according to Von Haxthausen.

11. Why did Russia sell Alaska?

12. How did the Slavophiles view the position of the Tsar in Russian society?

13. What, according to Herzen, facilitated the growth of the Russian radical movements? Was he correct?

14. What was the nature of Alexander III's government, according to Witte?

15. Why was the construction of the Trans-Siberian Railroad important to Alexander III?

16. What were the underlying problems between Russia and Japan, which led to the Russo-Japanese War?

17. Why did Pobedonostsev regard the press as a threat to the existing order?

18. Why did Witte and Stolypin want to save the monarchy through economic measures? In what ways did their measures differ?

19. What, according to Nicholas II, were Russia's aims in the First World War?

20. The ability to evaluate evidence on the basis of internal criteria is an essential part of the historian's craft. How reliable are some of the sources in this volume which might be biased or contain self-serving remarks made by statesmen, for example, who wish to justify or advance their careers?

Glossary

Desiatina   A measure of land (approxmately $2\frac{3}{4}$ acres).

Duna   Originally, the name of the Kievan boyar council. Later, the name of the elected legislative assembly or parliament during the reign of Nicholas II.

Mir   The ruling organization of the Peasant Commune; Peace; World.

Muzhik   A Peasant.

Obshchina   A Peasant Commune.

Bibliography

Section One

James F. Brennan, *Enlightened Despotism in Russia. The Reign of Elisabeth, 1741–1762* (New York, 1987).

Mina Curtis, *A Forgotten Empress. Anna Ivanova and Her Era. 1730–1740* (New York, 1974).

Basil Dmytryshyn, ed. *Modernization of Russia under Peter I and Catherine II* (New York and Toronto, 1974).

Vasili Klyuchevsky, Liliana Archibald, trans. *Peter the Great* (New York, 1958).

Philip Longworth, *The Three Empresses* (London, 1972).

L. Jay Oliva, ed. *Catherine the Great* (Englewood Cliffs, N. J., 1971).

Marc Raeff, *Peter the Great Changes Russia* (Lexington, Mass., 1972).

B. H. Sumner, *Peter the Great and the Emergence of Russia* (New York, 1962).

Section Two

Joseph T. Fuhrmann, *Rasputin* (New York, 1990).

Leopold H. Haimson, *The Russian Marxists and the Origins of Bolshevism* (Cambridge, Mass., 1955).

W. Bruce Lincoln, *The Great Reforms. Autocracy, Bureaucracy and the Politics of Change in Imperial Russia* (Dekalb, Illinois, 1990).

N. G. O. Pereira, *Tsar-Liberator: Alexander II of Russia, 1818–1881* (Newtonville, Mass., 1983).

Richard E. Pipes, ed. *The Russian Intelligentsia* (New York, 1961).

Marc Raeff, *Michael Speransky. Statesman of Imperial Russia, 1772–1839* (The Hague, 1969).

Nicholas V. Riasanovsky, *Nicholas I and Official Nationality in Russia, 1825–1855* (Berkeley, 1961).

Idem, Russia and the West in the Teachings of the Slavophiles (Cambridge, Mass., 1952).

Idem, A History of Russia Fourth Edition (New York, 1984).

Francis William Wcislo, *Reforming Rural Russia. State, Local Society, and National Politics, 1855–1914* (Princeton, 1990).